W9-CXT-134

THE TEACHING
OF
POPULAR DANCE

J. M. HODGES LIBRARY
WHARTON COUNTY JUNIOR COLLEGE
WHARTON, TEXAS

NEW DESIGNS IN
HEALTH, PHYSICAL EDUCATION AND RECREATION

ANN PATERSON, Ed. D., *Editor*

PROFESSOR OF PHYSICAL EDUCATION

SAN FRANCISCO STATE COLLEGE

NEW DESIGNS IN HEALTH, PHYSICAL EDUCATION AND RECREATION

THE TEACHING OF POPULAR DANCE

by

VIRGIL L. MORTON
SAN FRANCISCO STATE COLLEGE

Illustrated by Hilda Sachs

30469

J. LOWELL PRATT & COMPANY
Publishers   New York

J. M. HODGES L
WHARTON COUNTY JUNIOR COLLEGE
WHARTON, TEXAS

TO:

Priscilla Betty Morton

Copyright 1966 by
J. Lowell Pratt & Company, Inc.
Library of Congress Catalog Card Number: 66-29892
Published by J. Lowell Pratt & Company, New York
and on the same day by The Copp, Clark Company,
Toronto, Canada
COVER DESIGN BY JULIO GRANDA
PRINTED IN THE UNITED STATES OF AMERICA

793.33
M 846 t

30469

CONTENTS

PREFACE

Popular dancing affords one of the rare opportunities for young men and women to work together in a physical activity that is mutually pleasant and beneficial. The same dances may be used and taught in identical ways to beginning students at either high school or college levels. The dances presented in this book have proven their qualities and values over a period of many years and are likely to continue to remain popular in the future. While all popular dancing undergoes a slow process of changing, the basic principles and purposes are permanent. The person who learns to dance properly and skillfully when he is young profits from the experience throughout his entire life.

Dancing is an excellent medium for attaining the widely recognized and desired objectives of physical fitness, including rhythmic exercise of the entire muscular structure, increased respiration and circulation, flexibility, coordination, endurance and vigor, relaxation, and good posture habits. All may be acquired under pleasant conditions with agreeable companions, good music, without special clothing, and with a minimum of easily obtained equipment. This activity can be carried over into the everyday living habits and occupations of the participants without the necessity of supervision of adult instructors.

The shy student develops self-confidence and emotional stability; the extrovert learns to display and develop his talents in a creative and positive manner. All become considerate and more cooperative with their fellow students, and they learn to function in a normal, desirable, male-female situation.

Every generation has produced its share of novelty and fad dances that have been enthusiastically adopted by young dancers as being exclusively theirs. Such dance trends have always met with criticism and with accusations of being detrimental or immodest. The Waltz and the Polka, which are now thought of as being "charming, old-fashioned, and the quintessence of modesty," encountered the same reactionary hostility when they were first presented to the public. Most fad dances quickly fade from fashion. If one does endure it is because it has qualities that go deeper than mere surface sensationalism. Encourage young dancers to learn some of the fad dances which are an important part of their world. In the hands of a competent instructor, these dances can be a valuable tool when combined with the more traditional dances. Students frequently discover that the all around dancer who does both the trend dances and the traditional ones has more fun than those limited to only a single phase.

Young people are often admonished by their parents and their teachers to "stand up straight." Many have taken courses in body posture without permanent results. Perhaps the fault lies in the lack of incentive. Students of dance constantly deal with posture. While the instructor may not always place a strong emphasis on posture *per se*, he demands the correct placement and coordination of muscles and parts of the body that will result in good posture. By observation, students soon learn that the best dancers are those who hold their bodies correctly. In an effort to emulate the better dancers, they then correct their own posture. If the habit of correct posture can be maintained until it becomes permanent, the student attains a lifelong advantage.

Because music is such an integral part of dancing, the student of popular dancing broadens his knowledge and outlook toward the entire field of music.

Dancers derive more pleasure from learning with a group than by taking private lessons. As part of a group, they feel less self-conscious; have an opportunity to meet new friends and to dance with several partners; and to become more cooperative and tolerant with their fellow students. Through observation, students become aware of both good and bad qualities in dancing without these attributes being specifically brought to their attention by the instructor.

At the conclusion of the term of beginning popular dancing, it is hoped that the student will be sufficiently stimulated to progress to a more advanced class, or to carry his newly gained interest into one of the many other facets of the broad range of dance art.

Although the author has presented familiar material that has acquired a certain patina of tradition, he has endeavored to approach the subject from a viewpoint and attitude that has not been expressed in previous publications. It is hoped that the book will prove to be a helpful guide to all those who have an interest in disseminating the art of popular dancing, whether they are student teachers, recreation leaders, or professional instructors.

Use of this book

This book, THE TEACHING OF POPULAR DANCE, has been written basically as an aid to the instructor of classes of popular dancing at the high school and college levels. However, since all beginners of popular dancing need to acquire the same fundamentals of the art, the book can be useful to any age group. Senior citizen groups, recreation groups, and the serious individual can be aided from the material presented herein.

No attempt has been made to include more than the foundation figures for each dance, with suggested progressions for combining and building these basic figures into a practice sequence that will be pleasing and helpful to the student. As they acquire a stable foundation for each dance, encourage students to experiment in exploring new combinations and new rhythmic patterns. Dancing should be a *creative expression* a well as a satisfying physical stimulation. The experienced instructor keeps each dance within the traditional framework of styling and figures which have been established by custom; it is not necessary or desirable to create entirely new forms, but only to allow the student to discover for himself some of the many possible variations of dancing which have not been dictated by the instructor.

Although this book does not follow the customary teaching schedule suggested by most publications on the subject, the author has been extremely successful in retaining the interest and obtaining the maximum results from his students by generally following the order of dances as they appear in the text.

It is not necessary to teach dances in the chronological order in which they came into being. Young students prefer to begin with dances identified with their own age group. They enjoy a variety of dances rather than working on one dance until it becomes a chore. Devote the first several meetings of each group to relaxing the inhibitions of the students and aiding them to move in a relatively free and confident manner. Styling and perfection of technique comes about through constant review and repetition of each dance. Allow sufficient practice time in each meeting period to allow the students to repeat and explore all the figures and combinations offered during the actual teaching portion.

This book does not stress etiquette, but because it is an important part of group functioning each instructor can make a practical application of the basic rules of social conduct so they become a part of the course of popular dancing. The extent to which one emphasizes etiquette depends upon the individual desires of the instructor and the limitations of time. In all cases, the rules taught should be those which are realistic and practical to the community in which they will be used. To insist upon rules of etiquette that might be encountered only in European courts of royalty is not the most suitable formula for the majority of American needs.

The sounds of laughter and friendly discussion among students as they dance is a rewarding indication of the success of the instructor's achievement. Because dancing is a happy experience, conduct the class in a relaxed atmosphere so that faster learning takes place. If students are permitted to relax tensions and anxieties in a normal manner they tend to be more attentive and retentive during the intervals in which the teacher is lecturing or demonstrating. A dancing class conducted in an environment of funereal solemnity can never be very productive.

Each class has a personality of its own and may require a different teaching approach than a parallel class. Teaching plans made in advance may not always be suitable for the exact moment they are scheduled for use. A competent teacher wisely keeps a flexible attitude toward both teaching and planning, and suits the instruction to the immediate moment. The author hopes that the methods presented in this book will offer new approaches to the subject of teaching popular dancing. It is not intended to be an exacting dictum of teaching methodology.

Acknowledgments

In preparing for a career as a dancer and a teacher of dancing, it is inevitable that one encounters strong personalities who leave a permanent contribution and impression on one's life. Among those who have shared their knowledge of popular dancing with me have been: Arthur Soderstrom, founder of the Soderstrom School of Ballroom Dancing, in Denver, Colorado, who prepared me with a thorough background in the art of popular dancing; the late Cesar "Vanni" Vanoni, exhibition Tango partner to Mistinguett and Mata Hari, for revealing to me his expertness in the Argentine Tango; the late Carmen Miranda, and her sister, for their delightful instruction in the Samba, the popular dance of their native Brazil; Syvilla Fort and the staff of the Katherine Dunham School of Primitive Dance, and Lavinia Williams, director of the Haitian Institute of Folkloric Dance, for their careful instruction in the skills of Afro-Caribbean dancing.

I am immeasurably indebted to Ann Paterson, Chairman of the Department of Physical Education for Women at San Francisco State College, whose encouragement and assistance made this book a reality; and to Hilda Sachs whose charming drawings have added a vital visual dimension to this volume.

THE TEACHING
OF
POPULAR DANCE

CHAPTER ONE

AMERICAN POPULAR DANCING

A Brief History

The word *popular* may be defined as that "which is suitable or intended for the people at large." By implication, it also means "something which is subject to the fickle whims and dictates" of that same public. The dances which were classified as "popular" in colonial Amercia are certainly far removed from those danced in the current era.

It is an established fact that popular dances can rarely be dictated or created by one dancing master or by a dance organization, nor can their exact origin always be clearly traced. In general, American popular dances have, like Topsy, "jes' growed." If the dancing public likes a certain sequence, or perhaps only a part of it, they are quick to adopt it, and as prompt to discard it when it ceases to be a novelty. Few dances survive to become "classic," but when they do it is because they are flexible enough to be adapted to new musical trends and durable enough to withstand the shock of innovation imposed upon them by each new generation.

American popular dances, which have never been confined by rigid codes of tradition, reflect the kaleidoscopic tastes and social values of each period. Dancing has not always been accepted by all groups in America, and all dances have individually undergone periods of denouncement and censuring before being accepted as a part of the American dance culture.

In colonial Virginia, the fashions in dancing followed those established in England, and played an important part in the social life of the communities. In the homes of the wealthy landowners and in public taverns, such as the Raleigh Tavern in

Williamsburg, dancing parties produced sounds of laughter, music and gaiety which rang through the night.

The popular dances were the Quadrilles which had been used in the English and French courts, modified versions of the *French Minuet*, and a contra dance favorite, the *Sir Rodger de Coverly*, which later became simplified under the more familiar name of *Virginia Reel*. Dancing masters were employed to instruct the sons and daughters of the plantation owners in the social graces of the period as well as the steps of the popular social dances. It was considered a mark of provincialism not to be able to dance the current favorites.

In the New England colonies to the north, the Puritan religious leaders discouraged "mixed" dancing between men and women, yet recognized the value of "skipping and leaping in rhythm." Probably the best recorded denouncement against dancing in the Pilgrim colonies resulted from the arrest and trial of Thomas Morton. Morton, a fur trader and merchant, but not a Pilgrim, had assumed control of a colony at Mount Wollaston, Massachusetts, in 1625. Under his governorship, the name of the colony was changed to Merry Mount.

In sections of England, Morton's native home, it had been a tradition to erect a Maypole on the 1st of May, and to dance the ancient Morris dances around it. Because Morton and his colony followed the English custom, the Puritan authorities sent an expedition from Plymouth, in 1627, under the leadership of Miles Standish, to attack the colony and arrest Morton on charges of "bacchanalian friskings to pagan gods."

That was America's last Maypole for many years. Later, English settlers in more remote regions of the Appalachian mountains were unmolested in their observance of the rites of the Morris dances and the traditional folk dances. Many of the dance figures which they used later became the foundation for the *American Square Dance*, which some authorities consider to be a decadent form of the old European Quadrilles.

The political freedoms gained through the American and French revolutions influenced a more relaxed and independent disposition toward the social amenities in both the old and the new world. The *Square Dance* followed the westward migration and became an important part of the communal barn raisings, quilting bees, and corn huskings in every pioneer village, ranch, and mining camp. As soon as the Waltz and the Polka were introduced from Europe, they became standard favorites. Later couple dances included the *Redowa*, the *Mazurka*, the *Varsovienne*, and the *Badger Gavotte*. The fact that some of the dances varied from their European originals was due, primarily, to the less sophisticated environment in which they were performed. Dancing floors of packed earth or rough-hewn timber necessitated changes in styling and character somewhat removed from the finesse of movement conceded on the waxed and polished parquetry of mirror-bedecked, baroque ballrooms.

Some religious sects discouraged dancing to instrumental music but permitted the use of games performed to vocal recitations or songs. Familiar figures of the quadrilles and square dances were tolerated under the guise of Play-Party games.

Without purposeful intent, the Shakers added a unique and original contribution to American dance lore. The Shakers were a subdivision of the Quaker faith who had separated from the older church in a self-imposed adherence to total celibacy. Several communities existed in the New England states and in Ohio, Kentucky, and Indiana during the 19th century. Part of their religious ritual involved the use of strenuous dances and exercises designed to "shake sin (and tensions) away." The dances were vigorously performed to vocal songs, many of them meaningless syllabic utterances supposedly inspired by "divine tongues." The dances were not mere "shakings and quakings," but were established into set forms and sequences requiring exacting footwork and phrasing. People outside the sect adopted some of the dances and games. One of these was the children's singing game, *Looby-Lou*, which has remained a childhood favorite down to the present. In the 1950's, the same game became the inspiration for a popular community dance which gained adult favor in ballrooms under the name *Hokey Pokey*.

The dominating influence on what was later to become America's most original contribution to popular dancing was the strong rhythmic patterns of the music of the American Negro. These had been brought to the attention of the American public through the professional Minstrel Shows which developed as a part of American theatrical entertainment as early as the 1840's. Prior to that time, minstrel entertainments existed on the large Southern plantations in which wealthy owners organized the musical talents of their Negro slaves into entertainment spectacles for the benefit of the landowner's guests. In time, plantation owners began to vie with each other in ostentatious displays of vanity and companies of minstrel players were sent from Plantation to Plantation.

The Negro slaves based their amusements upon the rhythmic patterns from their native Africa, adding lyrics and dances in styles anticipated to please their masters. Some of the songs were the heartfelt laments of the displaced Negro; many were spirituals in which the fervor of both African and American religion became blended into a new and distinct musical form.

Professional entertainers who were privileged to see the Plantation diversions were quick to realize the new art form and to adapt it to their own usage. Although many were poor imitations or outright burlesques of the original shows, the unique musical rhythms were followed as closely as possible. Many professional shows employed Negro musicians, especially after the Civil War; others were white entertainers who performed their parodies with blackened faces. Minstrel shows formed the major substance of popular American theatrical performances during the late 1800's. Traveling companies exhibited their skill in the "opry houses" of every small community, and often in improvised theatres in remote cow towns and mining camps of the newly expanded western territories.

During the "gay '90's," which was in reality a period of financial depression and unemployment, the syncopated, scintillating music of the American Negro moved from the theatrical stage onto the floor of the ballroom. The "walkaround" dances, which were part of the Minstrel shows, lent their form to the new *Cake Walk* and the *Strut*, couple dances which encouraged creative improvization by the participants. The Waltz was influenced and altered into a more American form through the popularity of sentimental ballads sung and played in three-quarter time. In the late 1890's, the *Two-Step* became the popular dance favorite and the term "ragtime" was coined to identify the new and distinct musical style.

1900-1910: From the new "ragtime" rhythm, a mass of exhibitionistic dances evolved that were revolutionary to the accepted standards of the European dances. They bore names that were as fantastic as their style of performance, including: *Cubanola Glide, Grizzly Bear, Turkey Trot, Bunny Hug, Harem Glide, Ballin' the Jack, Camel walk,* and *Kangaroo Hop.* Some dances owed their place of birth to the colorful, but unsavory, environment of San Francisco's Barbary Coast, and New York's Bowery, but were readily accepted by novelty-seeking dancers in all strata of society. The new ragtime music and dances also encountered multitudinous expressions of disapproval and charges of creating libertine conduct by the moralists of the era.

Among the European importations which remained favorites in the ballrooms of the period were the *Three Step,* the *Valeta Waltz,* the *Rye Waltz,* the *Varsovienne,* and various interpretations of the *Schottische.* The popularity of the Square Dance declined to the extent that it almost vanished from the big cities and larger communities, and was contemptuously relegated to the status of backwoods dancing.

1910-1920: During the period of emotional stress created by America's involvement in World War I, popular dancing provided a welcome escape from war bulletins and the "fish bowl blues," a method of selecting military draftees by drawing names from a bowl. The afternoon Tea Dansant grew to the extent that all major hotels and ballrooms employed several orchestras; some playing throughout the evening and into the early morning hours. The *Fox Trot* was the dancing innovation which proved to be so popular it soon eclipsed most of the older forms.

The exhibition dance team of Irene and Vernon Castle played an important part in altering the style of American dancers into one which was more subdued and graceful. They were instrumental in introducing the *One-Step,* the *Hesitation Waltz,* the *Castle Walk,* and a practical, modified form of the *Argentine Tango* to American dancers.

Other dances popular during the decade were the *Toddle*, the *Waddle*, and the *Gabby Glide*.

1920-1930: This decade saw the birth of several teacher organizations which attempted to standardize the many forms of American popular dancing. The *Argentine Tango* was elevated to a zenith of popularity by the silent screen idol, Rudolph Valentino, who used it in several of his motion picture roles. "Jazz" became the term associated with the popular syncopated musical rhythms and with the dancers who followed those rhythms. Gilda Gray, a popular singer and dancer introduced the *Shimmy*, which became a popular figure in the Fox Trot. The *Charleston* introduced a new musical rhythm and style of dancing. Close imitations included the *Black Bottom*, *Sloppy Sailor Walk*, and the *Flea Hop*. The *Lindbergh Hop*, the *Varsity Drag*, and the *Hoosier Hop* came into being during the decade. Attempts to introduce the Spanish popular dance, *Paso Doble*, to the American public met with limited interest.

The "wireless" radio became an important feature of amusement and communication in most homes. It proved to be a boon to popular dancing by providing a constant barrage of current musical hits played by the most outstanding orchestras of the era.

1930-1940: Although the decade was marked by bank closures, calamitous crop failures caused by prolonged drought, and general unemployment, it was one in which dancing expanded into America's most popular activity. During this time the "big bands" competed with one another to create new methods of producing music which was distinct and original. The *Rumba* and *La Conga* brought Afro-Latin dance and musical forms to North American dancers. The acrobatic *Jitterbug*, and the more modified *Shag* both made their debut on dance floors across the nation. *Truckin'*, *Suzy-Q*, and the *Big Apple* challenged dancers to display their skills in creative pantomime. Marathon endurance contests attracted participants who were eager to provide public exhibitions of popular dancing. The contestants were frequently urged into joining these spectaculars by the economic necessity of gaining temporary employment and by vague promises of winning public adulation.

Sequence dances from England included *Boomps-a-Daisy*, the *Chestnut Tree*, and the *Lambeth Walk*. The *Carioca* was inspired by the motion picture dance team of Fred Astaire and Ginger Rogers. The introduction of several new musical compositions in the *Polka* idiom provided a reviving stimulant for that dance.

1940-1950: The G. I. Joes of World War II spread American popular dancing into remote corners of the world. A "new" method of accenting Fox Trot rhythm (actually a modified return to the old Ragtime) was termed "*Swing*," and the *Lindy*, *Shag*, and *Jitterbug* merged into one dance under that name. Carmen Miranda, an effervescent dancer from Brazil, promoted public interest in the Brasilian *Samba*. The *Mambo* grew out of the *Afro-Cuban* musical forms by injecting a syncopated accent; *Cha-Cha* emerged from one figure of the Mambo.

Teen-age dancers enjoyed the intricate footwork of the *Bop*, a dance inspired by a complex method of playing jazz termed be-bob, or re-bob, by musicians. The *Balboa* gained popular favor during the decade.

The high cost of amusement taxes imposed during World War II brought about such a serious decline in attendance at functions involving dancing that many ballrooms and clubs were forced to close. The same situation compelled the majority of the dance orchestras to disband by the end of the period.

1950-1960: Attempts to stimulate dance interest brought several new dances from the Caribbean islands, including: *Calypso*, *Pachanga*, *La Plena*, and *Merengue*. Most of them attracted only a limited segment of dancers. The *High Life*, from western Africa, suffered the same lack of interest. The *Bunny Hop* and the *Hokey Pokey* were audience participation dances which have remained useful as ice breakers and dance party stimulators.

Mashed Potatoes resembled the older Charleston. It was a favorite with teen-age dancers who danced it to the new Rock 'n Roll music, so named from the short phrases employed to produce a repetitive "rocking" rhythm. The most unique contribution of the decade was the *Twist*, which ushered in an entirely new conception of popular dancing.

1960-to date (1966): The majority of dances originated during the current decade have been distinct departures from the older, "classical" forms. They are performed, generally, in challenge position, and while most have been creations or inspirations of youthful dancers, a large number of adult emulators have been quick to adopt them. The dances use undulating rhythms which pass in throbbing, wave-like pulsations through the dancer's body and into sweeping arm gestures. The pelvic area employs free contracting and releasing movements. Some observers state that the current dances are a return to primitive forms.

The *Twist* started the trend. Others which have followed are: the *Swim*, the *Watusi*, the *Pony*, the *Frug*, the *Jerk*, *Hully Gully*, the *Surfer*, the *Hitchhiker*, the *Monkey*, the *Dog*. Some have enjoyed national popularity while others have been localized in their acceptance.

The music of the Bosa Nova originated in Brazil, being the Samba rhythm to which a jazz syncopation has been added. The dance of the *Bosa Nova* started in the United States and resembles a Rumba with a Twist influence. While it contains a potential for future development, it has currently failed to gain popular usage.

Although the popular dances of the present decade symbolize a revolt from the older forms, they may, in time, evolve into a structure as standardized and "classical" as the Waltz, the Fox Trot, or the Tango.

Dance Styling

Dance styling is that elusive combination of elements which aids in giving each dance its own personality and individual character. Because so many of the Amercan popular dances have been inspired by, or adapted from, those from other nationalities, the emotional, historic and sociological backgrounds of those countries have played an intrinsic part in creating "style" patterns. While it is not necessary, or desirable, to recreate totally the original dances in a true ethnic sense, the student who takes into sympathetic consideration some of the factors which have gone into the backgrounds of the dance becomes better qualified to achieve the correct styling than the one who merely stops with the external technique of the steps.

In the so-called Latin dances, including Rumba, Cha-Cha, and Samba, the manner of movement is due to a freer, more relaxed usage of the pelvic region than is normally the habit of the majority of North Americans. This same freedom *can* be achieved by simply *allowing* the abdominal and hip muscles to relax sufficiently to permit an undulating carriage of the pelvic bone. The tropical climate, also, influenced the native styling of these dances. Where temperatures and humidity percentages are consistently high, dancers tend to move in a more energy-conserving manner than do those in cooler climates. In the Samba, the practice of keeping the feet close to the floor originated with the type of slippers worn by the dancers, especially the women. These were of the type classified as "mules," a sole fitted to the foot by a narrow strap across the toes. Any uncontrolled, or kicking actions would quickly dislodge the slippers from the dancer's feet.

Geographically, the Argentine Tango is a "Latin-American" dance, but it does not follow the free use of the pelvis associated with other dances in that category. The characteristic styling of the Tango originated with the heavy garments worn by the Argentine Gaucho, the cowboy of the South American plains, and that of his dancing companion. The men's customary apparel consisted of a jacket ornamented with silver buttons, full trousers made of many layers of thick cloth, heavy leather boots adorned with large, silver spurs, and a wide leather belt which encased his waist. The ladies were gowned in full skirted dresses which were heavily ruffled in the fashionable mode dictated by the dress designers of Spain, the homeland of many of the Argentines. The quality of controlled, deliberate technique resulting from dancing in the cumbersome clothing created the "style" still emulated by contemporary dancers of the Tango.

The American Waltz has changed its style to a noteworthy extent from the rigid, military posture demanded by the original Viennese Waltz. The slower American tempo permits the dancer a more relaxed use of the knees and body to create flowing figures and footwork which would not have been possible in the faster-paced original.

Fox Trot and Swing are the only two dances of American origin which have endured the fickle fluctuations of dance fashions long enough to become "classic." Both dances have undergone considerable modifications from their original forms. Although certain patterns of footwork and styling characteristics have become well enough established to be considered foundation figures, the charm of both dances lies in their spontaneity and adaptability to improvization inspired by the many moods and qualities of the musical accompaniment. Generally, it is the tempo and rhythm of the music which determines the correct "style" for the Fox Trot and Swing. If the music is slow and sustained, the dancer's styling should follow the same pattern; when it is lively and effervescent the dance must reflect the same mood.

Conformity, to a limited degree, might be considered a part of "styling," also. If some dancers perform in such a manner that they are constantly a menace to their fellow dancers, they may then be considered "out of style."

The location of the dance and the manner in which the dancers dress will often play a part in dance style. Dancers tend generally to be more restrained and formal at a dance given in a ballroom of a fashionable hotel than they would be at an informal dance presented in the family rumpus room. Ballroom gowns and dinner jackets cause a more reserved manner than when the same people wear wash dresses or slacks.

CHAPTER TWO

THE TEACHING PLAN

The fault most frequently perpetuated by teachers of popular dancing is to assume that beginning pupils come to them already equipped with enough background knowledge to permit them to begin immediately working on figures of one of the traditional ballroom dances, usually one requiring closed position. This is the equivalent of a piano teacher assuming that a pupil can sit down and play a concerto on the premise that the pupil has experienced hearing others play; or the obsolete theory that a person learns to swim by being thrown into deep water.

All beginning students of popular dancing possess fears and inhibitions about learning an activity which is unfamiliar to them. The older the pupil, the greater his inhibitions will be. Among the self-conscious fears experienced by the novice will be his concern with:

(a) *MUSIC* — Although most of the young people in the United States have been subjected constantly to popular music from radio and television broadcasting, and possibly by concert and theatrical offerings, very few are aware that popular dancing is performed to the *base beat* of the music, and *not* to the *melody*. Many have to *"learn to hear"* the base rhythm in order to separate it from the melodic line.

They worry that they will not know "when to begin," or that they cannot keep time; some will profess to being "tone deaf."

(b) *FEET* — The most skilled athlete who is able to dart across a tennis or basketball court with remarkably deft footwork frequently discovers that those same feet turn to leaden weights upon first attempting to dance. All beginning dancers are concerned about appearing clumsy and awkward and fear they will stumble over the feet of their partners. They believe they will not be able to make their feet move in intricate patterns, and are convinced they will be expected to glide skillfully around the floor with the same ease and elan displayed by the professional performers seen on motion picture and television screens.

(c) *DANCING WITH A PARTNER* — Beginning dancers, regardless of age, are frequently embarrassed by having to hold, or be held, in the arms of another person. It is especially terrifying when neither partner knows the correct placement of hands, how far or near to stand, and even where to look.

By using the proper approach in the primary sessions of the term, the instructor can allay the natural concerns of the student and create an atmosphere in which the common purposes of both student and instructor will function in harmony. With the aid of some of the dances listed in the chapter on AUXILIARY DANCES, or by using similar ones, the teacher begins right away to aid the students to coordinate simple patterns of movement and footwork to music that is easy for them to hear and understand. Because detailed explanations are not necessary, a pleasant, relaxed atmosphere can quickly be established. Students soon realize that dancing can be fun, and not the dreary ordeal they had anticipated.

Swinging Mixer is a good beginning dance which does not require exacting footwork. The sequence is simple enough for any student who can count to eight. Because it is a mixer, it serves to acquaint students with one another, and as a group activity none needs to feel shy about participating.

Zorba the Greek creates a group feeling while easy footwork is being coordinated with a musical rhythm which is easily heard. It has the advantage of permitting everyone to participate without the necessity of having partners.

Although *San Francisco Stomp* is more complex than some of the introductory dances, beginning students appreciate the liberty it affords them to dance without physical contact with another dancer and to develop their own style of movement. In this respect it resembles many of the currently popular teen-age fad dances.

With these, or similar dances, students quickly learn to associate music and movement and then gradually advance to dances involving more difficult structures.

With the introduction of each dance, give students an opportunity to hear the music and become familiar with different methods of counting it. The teacher needs adequate musical training to be able to perceive and analyze the rhythms for the benefit of the students. Urge any student who intends to teach dancing to enroll in a class in musical analysis, or to learn through playing a musical instrument. While there is a vital partnership between music and dancing, a teacher must not permit the musical analysis to overbalance the instruction of dance skills.

As each dance is generally mastered, request the students to experiment freely in using new arrangements of the basic patterns and their variations. In some cases, the music may be used differently than had been demonstrated in the classroom. Base limitations upon the character and styling of each dance which has become traditional through popular usage. American popular dancing has always been noted for its spontaneous quality, a feature frequently misunderstood and envied by dancers from other countries. Spontaneous movement which is both inspired and disciplined can be developed by directing and encouraging students to use their creative imaginations productively.

The figures listed in this book must be considered only as the basic "ingredients" of each dance. When these have become understood, encourage students to add their own dash of "spice" to suit their individual tastes and personalities. Ideally, the good popular dancer is one who has gained enough self-freedom and flexibility in his dance movement to allow the music to dictate the sequence of the dance rather than to attempt to follow a set pattern of memorized steps. This is not meant to imply that the individual students should be permitted to operate on a mediocre, "anything goes" basis. All of the students' efforts must be subjected to the high standards maintained and practiced by an adequately informed and trained teacher of popular dancing.

Ear Training

Aural recognition of the many dance rhythms is an integral

part of learning to dance. As dance students become proficient enough to attend "dances" outside the classroom, they will be faced with the necessity of recognizing the music which is being played by the orchestra; rare, indeed, is the club or ballroom orchestra which announces the rhythm they will play. Part of the challenge of dancing is to be able to identify the music correctly.

Warn students against associating a specific rhythm with a specific melody. A competent musical arranger can use any melody, "Three Blind Mice," for example, and fit it to the rhythmic requirements of a Waltz, Cha-Cha, Rumba, or any other dance form. To a novice dancer who cannot distinguish rhythm, the transfer of a melody which may be familiar in one rhythm to that of another dance form can be perplexing.

The obvious method of helping students become aware of rhythm is to explain the basic rhythmic structure of each dance as it is introduced. By using the graphic musical diagrams presented in this book, the student can form a *visual* image of the musical structure and connect it to the aural rhythm. By tapping or clapping the rhythm of each new dance, students soon learn to distinguish the rhythm from the melody. As an instructor, be certain to use recordings in which the base section is musically well marked. Use a variety of recordings for each dance, played by different orchestras and at differing tempos. A repetition of one selection is not only monotonous but does not afford the student the fullest opportunity to recognize rhythms.

Do not expect beginning students of popular dancing to use musical counts and terminology in the same manner employed by a professional musician, however, the *net result should be the equivalent*. An instructor needs to use a variety of methods in counting music and footwork; permit each student to use whichever method has the most significance and clarity to him. All dancers need to learn to recognize the predominant "beat" in the music, and to distinguish 3/4 from 2/4 and 4/4 rhythm. Dancewise, both 2/4 and 4/4 rhythms are usually counted in multiples of 2, and for practical purposes may be considered to be the same. The principal difference lies in the tempo with which each is played, and therefore, becomes more of a concern to the musician playing the music than to the novice dancer attempting to distinguish the subtle musical values. In some dances, of which the Tango is an example, it is necessary to recognize the *musical phrasing* as well as the rhythm. In the Tango, the dance phrasing should correspond to the musical phrasing; in the majority of popular dances, the relationship is not so acute.

The rhythm section of an orchestra is made up of percussion instruments, and usually includes the stringed bass. These instruments produce a fundamental vibration which can be experienced physically by touching or standing near the speaker of the record player. Students who have genuine difficulty in distinguishing rhythms, or who confuse *melody* to mean *rhythm*, can benefit by placing their hands on the speaker of the sound reproducing instrument. They gain additional experience by trying the same experiment with their home television or radio equipment. Many people who are truly deaf are able to dance and enjoy music through the same principle of sensing vibrations created by sound waves.

Although some orchestral directors, at times, like to confound the dancer by playing a false introduction, once the musical rhythm has been established it continues throughout the selection without a change of time signatures. Occasionally, an orchestra retards or accelerates the rhythm toward the ending of a selection; dancers who have gained sufficient technical skill and musical perception enjoy the change of pace that such selections afford.

For most beginning dancers, the rhythms of the Latin-American dances are the most difficult. Because Latin-American orchestras use instruments which are not familiar to most North Americans, and because the musicians frequently *ad lib* their playing in counterpoint to the basic rhythm, it frequently requires more time for the novice to "hear" these rhythms than music with less complex structures.

One aid toward establishing recognition of the Latin rhythms is to devote proportionately more time to the study and analysis of the music than may be required for other forms. Assist the

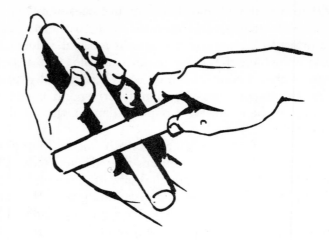

student in both aural and visual understanding of the rhythms by using the graphic musical analyses presented in this book. An additional benefit is for the instructor to emphasize the rhythm by using one of the instruments typical of Latin orchestras. The easiest to master are the *claves* (pronounced "CLA-vase"). Claves consist of two round sticks of hardwood, about eight inches in length. Hold one stick at one end by the thumb and forefinger and rest the other end upon the wrist. The palm of that hand is held in a semi-cupped manner to make a resonating chamber for the instrument (see illustration). When the clave is struck by the one in the other hand it produces a sharp, metallic sound which blends well with the music but is easily distinguished above the other sounds. A right-handed person usually cups the clave in the left hand and strikes it with the one held in the right hand, but it is not important which hand positions are used.

Claves may be obtained from, or ordered through, any dealer of musical instruments. The cost of the claves is nominal, and with care they will last many years.

One can use a wood block or a small drum in place of the claves. A hand-clapped rhythm produces a negative reaction from students if it is used frequently.

After becoming familiar with the basic rhythms of the dances and learning to employ them as guides to footwork and movement, students must also learn to be aware of, and react to, the multiplicity of moods and images evoked by the music. If the music is soft and romantic in nature, the dancer's movements should reflect a similar quality; when the music is blatant and animated, dancers should respond with equal vigor.

Speed of Teaching

The number of hours allotted to the teaching program determines, to a large extent, the number of dances which may be introduced during a semester. The more frequently a class meets, the more material students retain without extensive reviews. If two hours per week are devoted to classwork, *two* one-hour periods are better than *one* two-hour period. The ideal situation is to have *three* one-hour sessions equally spaced throughout the week.

It is not necessary to bring to a high polish and master completely each dance before the next one is introduced. Students enjoy the challenge and the variety offered by working on more than one dance during the same period. Strive to use dances of different styles and tempos so that they do not become merged in the minds of the inexperienced students.

Conduct each meeting at a lively pace by keeping *all* students active. Students need to realize that they are working in a group situation in which no *one* pupil occupies a large block of the instructor's attention. *Direct corrections to the entire group, not to each individual student.* Maintain a pleasant, positive, and congenial attitude in the classroom at all times.

Among beginning dancers, the women may appear to learn at a faster rate than the men. The illusion is caused, in part, by the fact that the men are required to think "double" — for themselves as well as for their partners. The instructor who gears the teaching speed to that which can be absorbed and put into practice by the men will find it is the correct pace for the group. No two classes respond in the same manner or work at exactly the same tempo. The instructor needs to work toward the requirements of each individual group. Allow sufficient practice time to have the students gain a firm grasp of the material presented during each meeting. Under the proper instruction and supervision, dancing is an activity in which "practice makes perfect."

Partners

When it is possible to do so, maintain an equal enrollment between the male and female students taking part in the class. This way everyone can participate in the learning of the fundamental steps at the same time.

Because each man leads in a slightly different manner, and each lady responds in her own way, make frequent changes of partners. The objective desired is to teach each partner to dance with *any* other partner, in *any* dance, in *any* situation, at *any* time. Two beginning students who dance together all the time before they acquire the essential skills often develop incorrect dancing habits that are not easily changed.

In groups with more women students than men, repeat each exercise and dance having the men change partners to enable the extra ladies to gain equal experience. While it is valuable for a lady to know the basic footwork used by both men and women, and to recognize the problems presented in leading, ladies in the primary stages of learning should concentrate upon the technique of following a male partner rather than attempting to lead another lady.

Demonstrating

The adage that "a picture is worth a thousand words" can appropriately be applied to demonstrating basic footwork and figures in popular dancing. If the teacher has an assistant, patterns and combinations to be demonstrated to the group should be discussed and rehearsed, if necessary, before the class meets. When a teaching assistant is not available, the instructor displays the finished figure by using one of the students in the class as a partner *after* the individual footwork and technique have been taught to the entire group. Use a different student-partner for each figure or combination demonstrated.

In demonstrating with a partner, the instructor first walks through the figure using a slow count after having first indicated the correct hand positions, styling, directions of movement, or other technicalities that aid the student to visualize each part. Then repeat the figure several times using music played at the desired tempo.

Clothing

Although dancing is an activity in which participants sometimes perspire freely, most students prefer to attend class in their normal school clothing. In this event, *insist* that clothing be clean and comfortable. Some schools require students to wear specific clothing for activity classes, in which case the instructor will be responsible for supervising the local precept.

Street shoes with leather soles are the best footwear for popular dancing, but their use may also be regulated by local school rules, the type of floor covering on the dancing area, or by miscellaneous other factors.

Texts and References

Each instructor decides whether he will require each individual student to have a textbook on popular dancing. If a text is not used, see that the school library has sufficient reference and background material for all the students.

Minimum Facilities

Keep the dancing area cheerful and well ventilated. Avoid cement or tile floors, if possible. The lack of resilience in such floors can be detrimental and fatiguing to the feet and legs of the students and instructor as well.

Use a sound system which provides clear, high fidelity reproduction of commercial recordings. If possible, it should be equipped with tone and speed controls. Because dancing is performed to the base rhythms, it is sometimes necessary to emphasize that part of the music by adjusting the tone control. Not all recordings are made at a tempo ideally suited to the instructor's immediate teaching needs; a tempo correction can be made by adjusting the speed of the turntable. If the speakers can be separated from the turntable, put them in a pre-tested location which provides the most advantageous sound coverage to the dancing area. Place the turntable in a location readily accessible to the instructor.

For the best sound reproduction, change the stylus frequently and see that a competent electrician checks the equipment at regular intervals.

Unless the size of the dancing area demands the use of a microphone, do not use one. Students respond better and feel a more personal contact with a voice that is not electrically amplified. If a microphone is necessary, learn the proper technique of using it.

Because of the necessity of amplifying the music, and possibly the instructor's voice, the space used as a classroom for popular dancing should be located either in a separated area or used at a period when the resulting sound will not be disturbing to pupils or teachers in surrounding classrooms.

Evaluation

Among the factors used in evaluating the progress of students in a class of popular dancing should be these:

(a) Attendance;

(b) Skills tests, by instructor, of basic steps and variations. Progress in skills achieved over a period of time. Student's ability to identify and "count" the basic rhythms of the dances taught;

(c) Cooperation with fellow students as evinced in willingness to change partners. Graciousness of the more advanced students in assisting those with less skill.

Selecting A Record Library

The selection of good music for popular dancing is vital to good teaching. The music must be played by a dance orchestra which provides even, well-defined accents distinct enough for the beginning dance student to hear without effort.

The majority of current recordings heard on radio and sold in record shops are not played by dance orchestras. Vocal soloists, vocal groups, and popular instrumentalists are frequently more interested in displaying their technical virtuosity than in adhering to a strict dance rhythm. Unless one is familiar with a record or record album, and can order by label name and number, record shop personnel are discouragingly uncooperative in assisting the teacher in selecting suitable recordings for dance music. Browsing and listening has become an affair of the past in modern record shops.

Fortunately, a number of companies do exist which specialize in the production of records for popular dance. All recordings are carefully pre-checked for rhythm and tempo by authorities who are experienced in the field of popular dance. Most selections are played by full orchestras, and each record is correctly marked as to whether it is a Waltz, Cha-Cha, Tango. Many even indicate the metronome count.

A post-card request to any of the following firms for its catalogue will also put a teacher on the mailing list of subsequent releases:

COMMAND RECORDS, 1501 Broadway, New York, New York, 10036;

DANCE ALONG RECORDS, 111 W. 57th Street, New York, New York, 10019;

HOCTOR RECORDS, P.O. Box 38, Waldwick, New Jersey, 07463;

ORION RECORDS, 614 Davis Street, Evanston, Illinois;

ROPER RECORDS, 4348 4th Street, Long Island City, New York, 11104;

TWELGRENN INC., P.O. Box 16, Bath, Ohio;

WINDSOR RECORDS, 5530 No. Rosemead Blvd., Temple City, California.

While it may seem impracticable to order records "sound unheard" from a catalogue, the teacher may be assured that most of them will be extremely satisfactory, and that all will be danceable. A special price rate is offered to instructors teaching in established studios and schools.

The instructor's library should include a good selection of each type of popular dance in slow, medium, and fast tempos. The standard melodies are the most satisfying and esthetically durable for the older dances, but for the novelty and discothéque dances the latest current releases are more suitable. Most young dancers like to identify with that which is currently popular and a good dance library should include a few recordings of this type. Discard the record as soon as it has ceased to be popular and replace it by a more current one.

Physically, records will last a long time with proper care. By keeping the records in their original paper jackets, or by placing them in albums, the playing surfaces will be protected from rubbing together and defacing the microgrooves. The correct playing stylus should be used and frequently changed. A scratched, distorted record is distasteful and annoying, and should be discarded or replaced.

Graphic Musical Analysis

If all dancers were required to study musical notation and analysis before enrolling in a dance class, it might lessen the burden of the instructor, but the condition would certainly curtail the interest of the usual student. As an aid to students of popular dance who are not familiar with musical notation, the author has devised a system of diagramming basic rhythms to serve as a *visual* link in relating the music with the footwork of each dance. Even the most intellectual musician needs to learn to respond *physically* to rhythms to enable him to become a good dancer. Although the notation system is not adequate for recording subtle nuances, it serves to illustrate visually the rhythmic basis of most popular dance music.

The circle, ◯, indicates one unit of time, or one "beat" of music. The circle has no specific meaning and *should not be confused* with a *whole note* used in traditional musical scoring. The circles may be replaced by any other objects such as apples, building blocks, or milk cartons, and employed in the same manner. When *one* circle, or any substitute object, is cut into two equal parts, *two* small equal pieces result. The same is true in music. By cutting one *long* note (comparatively) into two parts, two *short* notes will be formed. The footwork follows the same arrangement; one *slow* step (comparatively) can be divided into two *quick* steps. A circle which has been divided by a heavy line, ⊕, indicates that the count, or beat, has been divided into two parts. The number of circles between each two parallel lines indicates the number of counts, or beats, in each measure of music. As an example, two measures of basic Cha-Cha rhythm and accompanying footwork are diagrammed:

Time Signature 4/4								
Count	1	2	3-&	4	1	2	3-&	4
Rhythm	S	S	Q-Q	S	S	S	Q-Q	S
Steps	L	R	L-R	L	R	L	R-L	R

A shaded circle, ⊛ , shows the count in the measure which receives the stressed *accent*. Timewise, it has the same value as the other whole circles in the measure. A two-measure diagram of the Waltz indicates its use:

3/4						
Count	1	2	3	1	2	3

By drawing each diagram upon the chalkboard, or by using a previously prepared chart and referring to it as the music is first played and analyzed, and again when the basic footwork is being introduced, the instructor assists beginning dance students to form quickly and easily a *visual* and *aural relationship* between the musical rhythm and the foot and body movements of each dance.

DANCE POSITIONS

Closed Position

The standard position used for the majority of traditional popular dances originated with the Austrian version of the Waltz. Regardless of the dance in which it is used, it may still be termed "Waltz" position, but it is more commonly referred to as "closed" or "ballroom" position. The position is fairly flexible with allowable adjustments to suit the style and physical demands of each dance, but exaggerated or affected positions must never be assumed.

Common sense and the comfort of the dancers dictate correct closed position (see illustration). Both dancers begin by standing comfortably erect to face their partner, with the lady *slightly*

to the man's right. Each person maintains his own weight without leaning upon the other for support. The body weight of each dancer should be brought forward sufficiently to place the body weight over the balls of the feet. Lifting the abdominal muscles prevents dancers' hips from sagging backward and also aids in maintaining a good, but relaxed, dance posture.

The man places his right hand behind the lady's back in a general area between her waistline and below her left shoulder blade. The exact position varies according to the size and height of each partner. Because the man uses his right hand to lead his partner, it will be necessary for him to move it from place to place to provide the best leverage for turning and directing her. It is rarely necessary, or desirable, for the man to completely encircle the lady with his arm.

The lady places her right hand in the man's left hand. The man's left arm and the lady's right arm must be comfortably extended to the man's left, elbows turned downward and clasped hands held approximately at the man's shoulder level. Some figures require the lifting or lowering of the clasped hands to accent the body line of the dancers, but, in most instances, the arms remain in the same position without extraneous motions. Enough muscular tension must be retained in the outstretched arms of both dancers to permit the man to initiate a strong lead with his left hand and to allow the lady to perceive and react to his lead. *All* closed position dances use the same extended arm position.

The lady places her left hand on the man's right shoulder. Through her hand she can sense the leading motions of his body. She must be careful not to let the hand slip downward to rest upon the man's elbow. This would cause the man to be thrown off balance in such a manner that he would find it difficult to lead.

The exact distance between partners depends upon the individual dance and upon a particular figure in each dance. The position must always be comfortable for both partners. Dancing at a full arm length is equally as bad form as encasing one's partner with a python's embrace.

Promenade Position

Promenade position is a variation of the traditional closed

position. The same hand hold is retained as that used in closed position, but both partners turn toward their clasped hands so that they are in a side by side position (see illustration). The specific figure being used dictates the degree of the opening. Promenade position is frequently used in Tango and the Samba; but rarely in the Fox Trot.

Open Position

Open position is basically the same as Promenade Position except that the clasped hands are released. The free arms and hands must not hang limply by the dancer's side, but must be used in a manner to complement the movement of the dance. In *Reverse* Open Position, partners turn in place against the line of direction to bring the man's left side and the lady's *right* side together. Open Position and Reverse Open Position are frequently used in Rumba, Samba, Cha-Cha, and some figures of the Tango.

Challenge Position

Partners begin facing each other; one or both hands may be extended to those of the partner, or, if the dancers desire, they may eliminate hand contact completely. Challenge Position allows both dancers unusual freedom in that they do not have to be using identical footwork as long as their basic rhythm is together. Both dancers need to develop free and interesting patterns of spatial movement around their partners and not limit their steps to those which simply move together and apart. Both partners must strive to dance as one unit, rather than as two solo dancers. Challenge Position is popular in Cha-Cha, Rumba, Samba, and Swing (in which a hand hold must be retained).

Varsovienne Position

Varsovienne Position derives its name from an old Polish ballroom dance. In Varsovienne Position, both partners face a common direction. The lady stands in front of the man and slightly to his right; he holds her right hand in his right hand, and her left hand in his left and at a comfortable position above her shoulder level (see illustration). This position may be used

for the Polka, and as a transitional position in the Samba and the Rumba.

Shoulder-Waist Position

In Shoulder-Waist Position, dancers stand face to face with their partner. The man places both hands around the lady's waist; she places her hands on the man's shoulders (see illustration). The Polka, and occasionally the Samba and Rumba make use of Shoulder-Waist Position.

Skating Position

Skating Position is rarely used in popular dancing except for the Polka. Partners face in the same direction; the man holds the lady's right hand in his right hand, and her left hand in his left hand. They hold the crossed hands downward at about waist level (see illustration).

THE MAN MUST LEAD

A man may know a thousand fancy variations and be able to perform elaborate ballroom gyrations, but unless he can convey those actions to his partner in a manner she can understand and follow, he is not a good dancer. Dancing is a partnership which two people share equally, but the *man* is the one responsible for making the decision as to which figures he and his partner use.

A good dancer is one who directs his partner with strong, decisive leading movements through the basic figures and variations of a dance while adhering to the correct styling and musical rhythm. Although the figures need to be varied enough to keep the dance from becoming monotonous, the man must not attempt to rival the professional exhibition dancers who perform elaborately choreographed and rehearsed routines. In the United States, popular dancing has always been spontaneous and creative, although a basic precept of foot patterns, styling and rhythm is generally followed to lend identity to each of the dances.

In contemporary popular dancing, two basic positions are commonplace; *Challenge position,* and *Waltz position.*

(a) *Challenge* position is one in which dancers stand in an open position facing their partner. (This is described on p. 27.) They may extend one or both hands across to hold the hand, or hands, of the partner; or they may release their hands without contact with the partner.

When partners join one or both hands, the man *must* lead his partner by strong movements in his arms to pull her toward him, to push her away, or to lead her into patterns of movement around him.

When hands are released, the lead becomes a *visual* one in which the man's steps and actions serve as the guiding signal to the lady. Since there is no physical bond between the dancers, they are both free to move in their own choice of spatial patterns around one another. The *visual* lead requires the establishment of a mental rapport between the two dancers which is usually not achieved without having danced together before.

(b) *Waltz* position, or more frequently termed "closed" position, is used for most traditional, popular dances. In the standard hold, the man places his right hand behind the back of his partner; his left hand extends outward to the side holding the lady's right hand (see section p. 23 on POSITIONS). Technically, the closed position, with its variations, is more difficult than Challenge position.

Upon taking a lady into closed position, the man acquires an additional pair of feet and legs which he must make respond to the exact counter-movements of his own. Communication to the new set of feet cannot be made verbally, but only by the correct use of the man's hands and body. He must push, pull, and turn his partner, the owner of those additional feet, to direct her forward, backward, and sideways. While first learning to dance in closed position, the man must not be timid in the use of his hands and arms. His partner *wants* to receive his directions through decisive, definite movements made by his hands and body. After both dancers have developed some skill, the leading gestures become more subtle but must always remain definite.

Both hands must be used in leading.

The man does not place his *right* hand around the lady's waist as a romantic gesture. It is there for *pulling* the lady forward, *pushing* her backward, and *turning* her to one side. Do not keep the right hand in one spot, but move it to whichever location seems most suitable for indicating the desired direction of movement. At times, the pressure exerted by the tips of the fingers is enough to indicate the lead to the lady; for other leads the man needs the heel of the hand, the entire hand, or the *hand plus the arm.*

The man uses his *left* hand and arm in very much the same manner. Although his hand generally remains clasped with the lady's right hand, he uses it to push or pull to indicate the direction he wants to go. The man relaxes his left arm into a comfortable curve, but he maintains enough muscular tension to make the leads positive and strong.

Not only does the man use his hands and arms in leading, but the *entire body* moves as well. The body must move with a sense of unity in which all parts coordinate toward leading the lady into the proposed directions and patterns. She, in turn, senses the man's "body lead" through her hands.

A good leader learns to *anticipate* the moves he wishes to make so that he may communicate them to his partner before the action takes place.

Various factors slightly alter the man's method of leading. Each dance has a different style, and this may determine the lead; each partner responds in a different way and this sometimes necessitates varying approaches in leading.

Learning to lead strongly and well cannot be accomplished instantly. It requires practice and patience, confidence in one's self, and willingness to apply each point as it is disclosed.

The following list of suggestions will aid men in developing a strong lead and to become good dancers:

1. Know the step patterns before attempting to lead. In addition to practicing in the classroom, practice the basic footwork of each dance without a partner, and in private, until the footwork becomes second nature. Use the cor-

rect music for each dance and follow the rhythm carefully. During the practice, think about the "extra pair" of feet which have to be made to respond to the lead.

2. In all dances, keep the weight slightly forward on the balls of the feet. Never allow the weight to settle back on the heels.

3. Keep the feet close together in moving forward or backward. The inside soles of the shoes may almost touch as they pass. Never dance in a "straddle" position.

4. Good posture is important. It does not mean the ram-rod stance used in military establishments, but a normal, comfortable body carriage gained through proper exercise and everyday habits of standing properly. A tall man must not stoop to accommodate a short lady, let her reach up to him.

5. Balance and lightness in dancing are frequently achieved by controlling the muscles in the middle part of the body. A man who sags in the middle will be heavy and unable to respond with the quick, decisive movements that characterize a good dancer.

6. Take time to listen and properly identify the music before beginning to dance. Do not become so involved in thinking about the footwork that the music is ignored.

7. When dancing with a new partner, begin with uncomplicated footwork. Both partners need to become accustomed to the "style" of the other person and to sense their dancing abilities.

8. The man is responsible for leading his lady safely through the traffic created by the other couples on the ballroom floor. He cannot guide his partner properly if he watches his own feet or those of other dancers.

9. For all closed position dances, the man *always* takes his *initial* step with his *left* foot.

10. Be a pleasant, expressive leader. It is not necessary to know a multitude of "steps"; the man who can combine familiar figures in an interesting, creative manner will be considered a good dancer!

THE LADY MUST FOLLOW

All too frequently, women tend to believe the only requirement necessary to make them a good dancer is to have a male partner who can lead her through a series of rehearsed footwork!

In the United States, dancers have always favored the free improvization of dance figures based upon footwork and styling which has been established by tradition. The basic figures and their variations are *not* put together in any set order, but vary with the whims and skills of the *leader* as well as the *mutual abilities of both partners.* The best male dancer in the world cannot lead a lady through the most simple figures with any degree of satisfaction to either partner unless the lady has a basic knowledge of the techniques of popular dancing. For this reason, the lady must be as well versed as her partner in the basic steps of all of the standard dances. Experienced men dancers frequently create variations of the basic footwork, but the lady who has also gained some experience does not find the variations difficult to follow.

In all dances using *closed* position, the man's lead to the lady is a *physical* one. It is indicated, generally, by leading movements of the man's hands in which he pushes or pulls her hands or her body to tell her the desired direction of movement. At the same time, he uses his body in such a manner that it points to his changes of direction. A good partner becomes sensitive to the leading indications which her male partner gives either by his hands or by his body. With a few rare exceptions, the lady always dances the exact counterpart to the man's steps in closed position dances.

The lead employed in dances which use the open *challenge* position is a *visual* one. Although the lady does not need to follow his identical footwork, she must permit the man to establish the character and mood they will use in common.

The following suggestions assist ladies toward becoming good dancers and good partners:

1. Practice the basic footwork patterns of the dances with-

out a partner, but to music. Make certain that the rhythm and the footwork are together. Practice the steps moving backward, forward, and to the side. Maintain a good posture and use the arms as if they were being held by a partner. Do not "over-practice" to the extent of developing set patterns of movement.

2. With a partner, use the hands and arms properly. In the traditional closed position, the lady's *left* hand rests firmly on, but not gripping, the man's right shoulder. If the man leads properly, the lady feels part of his leading movements being transmitted through his shoulder. Never *lean* upon that shoulder; to do so would throw the man off balance to the extent that he could travel only in a small circle. The man's clasped left hand holds the lady's right hand. It is important for the lady to maintain enough tension in her *right arm* and *elbow* to permit her to perceive and react to the pushed or pulled lead indications given by the man; do not let the arm become a "Raggedy Ann" one.

3. The lady must literally "stand on her own feet" and not use her partner as a "prop" to lean against, or to hang around his neck.

4. Generally, make all steps with long, free movements originating from the hips. Ladies frequently accuse a man of stepping on her toes when they may have been at fault by having made a step which was too short.

5. Good posture is imperative, but it must be a normal posture which has been developed from daily habits of exercise and by consistently standing erect and proud. If a lady happens to be taller than her dancing partner, she must not stoop to accommodate him; let the man reach upward.

6. Relax, mentally and physically, and *let* the man be responsible for leading. *Do not anticipate* his lead before he has given it.

7. Some dances require different "styles" of footwork. Learn to use the feet properly for the dance being performed. Most closed position dances require the "dancers' walk,"

in which the toe of the foot is touched to the floor before the heel is brought down. The rule applies whether the direction of movement is forward, backward, or sideward. The free foot always passes close to the standing foot; never let the feet separate into a wide "straddle" position.

The footwork used for the Latin-American dances has a more "earthy" quality. The feet are placed upon the floor in a more "flat" manner, but they must retain a lightness which must not become coarse or cumbersome.

For both styles, the dancer keeps his weight on the front part of the feet and *never* shifts it backward to remain over the heels.

8. Even in figures requiring a "visual" lead, a lady must not develop a habit of watching her partner's feet or her own. Learn to respond to the directions communicated by the man.

9. The secret of "balance" and "lightness" lies in the use of the muscles in the mid section of the body. A dancer needs to learn to control those muscles by tensing or relaxing them in the proper amounts at the correct time. They must be used with *"controlled relaxation"*; never pulled inward too tightly and never allowed to sag in a totally relaxed manner.

10. Because each man leads a bit differently than another, and because he will use his own choice of combinations and variations, ladies must gain as much experience as possible by dancing with many men. By dancing with one partner for a prolonged length of time, one establishes improper habits of following which are difficult to remedy.

Be a pleasant, cooperative partner and enjoy the reputation of being a good dancer by being a good follower!

TERMINOLOGY

In working with beginning dancers in high school and college classrooms, the instructor should strive to use directional and uncomplicated terminology. If each term is explained as the teacher encounters it the students will readily associate the terms with the actions or positions to which they apply. The practice in general use in the professional popular dance studios of applying an elaborate name to each simple variation of a basic figure is not feasible in a school situation where the teaching program is limited by a time schedule. Not all terms are standard throughout the United States. If other terminology is more familiar in certain areas, the instructor should feel at liberty to substitute the local term.

In using reference material originating in other countries, the instructor will find that systems of notation and terminology greatly vary from those used in the United States. Even the terms listed here are general and differ slightly as they are applied from one dance to another.

ACCENTED BEAT — an additional force placed on certain pulse beats of a series. For example, a waltz rhythm count 1 is accented to distinguish it from counts 2 and 3. (Also see Beat.)

BALANCE STEP — a controlled shift of weight from one foot to the other, either forward, backward, or sideward. It may be used in all ballroom dances.

BASIC FIGURE — all standard dances have an established combination of steps, or foundation figure, identified as the "basic figure."

BEAT — the rhythm established by a mathematical sequence of intervals of time, or pulsations. These are established in the base section of an orchestra with the use of percussion and brass instruments. Ballroom dancing is always danced "on the beat" and not to the melody. In some dances, such as the Tango, the melody does serve as a guide in grouping a number of "beats" to form a sequence, or figure, in the dance pattern.

BOX STEP — a figure common to all ballroom dances in which the feet move through a square or "box" formation. The figure, also known as the "Square Step," will vary in its formation from dance to dance.

CHALLENGE POSITION — one in which the dancers stand generally

face-to-face without holding hands as they dance. It is frequently used in many of the "Latin" dances, and in the contemporary
fad dances. The terms "Conversation position," and "Separation
position" are also used.

CHASSÉ — literally meaning "to chase." A sliding step in which
one foot displaces the other as if by chasing it. It may move forward, backward, or sideward. In American Square Dancing, the
term has been corrupted to "Sashay." Technically, it is a series
of gliding steps taken in the desired direction alternately closing
the second foot to the leading one.

CLOCKWISE — in the direction in which the hands of a clock rotate; to the *right*. It is applied to either couples or individuals
turning, or a path of direction in which the dancers move.

COUNTERCLOCKWISE — in the direction *opposite* to that in which
the hands of a clock rotate; to the *left*. The term may be applied
to either couples or individuals turning, or to a patch of direction. In dances such as the Waltz, Fox Trot, and Tango, the flow
of the movement of the dancing couples is always *counterclockwise* around the dancing area.

DANCE WALK — similar to a natural walk but with the toe touching the floor first instead of the heel. It may move either forward,
sideward, or backward in such dances as Tango, Waltz, and Fox
Trot.

DISCOTHÉQUE — a word borrowed from the French, literally
meaning "a place where records (disques) are stored." It has
become the term to describe a place where popular dancing is
performed to records rather than to a live orchestra.

DOWNBEAT — originally applied to the downward motion of a
conductor's hand, but is also loosely used to mean any accented
beat in music.

FIGURE — a combination, or sequence, of steps that make a pattern. Frequently termed "step," as with "Waltz step."

FOLLOW THROUGH — a point in good styling in which the free foot
passes close to the standing foot while leading into a step for-

ward or backward. This prevents the "straddling" effect which results from keeping the feet too far apart while dancing.

HESITATION — a figure which is held in place for two or more counts after making the initial step in any direction, such as Waltz Hesitation.

LINE OF DIRECTION — the counterclockwise line of movement around the dancing area used in such dances as Waltz, Fox Trot, Tango.

OPEN POSITION — (see Promenade Position) evolves from Promenade Position. Dancer's clasped hands (man's left, lady's right) are released to move freely. Inside hands may be held, or man may retain his hold with his right hand behind the lady's back; she keeps her left hand on the man's shoulder. The position may also reverse to move in the opposite direction.

PHRASE — there are musical phrases and dance phrases. The *musical* phrase is expressed in the melodic line and can be compared with a spoken sentence in that it conveys an idea or thought. The musical phrase may vary in length. The *dance* phrase is a chain of steps that constitutes a figure. The musical phrase and the dance phrase need not always coincide in contemporary ballroom dancing.

PROMENADE POSITION — develops from closed or Waltz position as both dancers turn forward into semi-open position. The hands retain the same general hold as in the closed position, but with adjustments to allow freedom in the more open position.

ROCK 'N ROLL — "country and western" music, and folk-blues music is usually composed in short musical phrases. By applying the same technique used in "swing" music of shifting the accents to the 2nd and 4th beats, and stressing those accents, the resulting rhythm is one that "rocks and rolls." There is no dance termed "Rock 'n Roll," but all of the contemporary fad dances are performed to this type of music.

SHOULDER-WAIST POSITION — with partners facing, the man places both hands around the lady's waist; the lady places both hands on the man's shoulders. Arms are held fairly straight. May be used in Polka and Samba, but rarely in other popular dances.

SLOW — a comparative term used in timing. A *slow* step, or count, takes the same amount of time as two *quick* steps, or counts.

SPOT DANCE — a dance performed in a small space without progressing around the dancing area. Cha-Cha and Swing exemplify *spot* dances.

SPOTTING — a term borrowed from ballet terminology used as a device to avoid dizziness resulting from a series of fast turning or pivoting figures. The dancer focuses his eyes upon one spot for as long as possible so that the head turns at a slower rate of speed than the body.

STEP — a term with two meanings: (a) a total transfer of weight from one foot to another. (b) a series of steps that makes up a figure of a dance, such as *Waltz Step.*

STEP IN PLACE — a series of changes of weight in which one foot returns to its original location several times.

STYLE — the characteristics associated with a particular dance through tradition or dictated by its source of origin.

SUPPORTING FOOT — foot upon which there is weight, as opposed to *free* foot. Also termed *standing* foot.

SWING — (a) a name of a dance derived from combining Jitterbug, Jive, and the Lindy Hop, and danced to *swing* music. (b) a method of producing a rhythm with a "swinging" effect by shifting the musical accents to the 2nd and 4th beats of popular music originally used for the Fox Trot. (c) a couple turn in place, frequently employed in Square Dancing, but seldom used in ballroom or popular dancing.

SYNCOPATION — a displacement of the normal accent of music. All forms of Jazz music use this.

TAP — see Touch.

TEMPO — speed of music as measured by a metronome.

TIME — the number of beats in each bar of music. 2/4 time has 2 beats per bar; 3/4 time has 3 beats per bar; 4/4 time has 4 beats per bar.

TOUCH — a touch or tap of the free foot to the floor, usually near the arch of the supporting foot.

TRIPLET — a smaller, faster version of the two-step. Used in Swing and Cha-Cha.

TURN(s) — in popular ballroom dancing, implies a series of steps, based upon a box, or square, sequence employed to change directions in place. Turns may be done to the left or to the right, and may be a complete (360 degree) revolution, or any fraction thereof. Although a change of direction can be effected by using a series of steps to make a small *circle* in place, it should not be confused with the "turn" employing the box, or square figure. The technique of the "turn" will vary according to the box figure used in each dance.

TWO-STEP — name of a dance and also a step pattern used in many dances. It consists of three changes of weight made within two beats of music.

VARIATION — a change from the foundation pattern of a dance, or from the basic rhythm of the music.

VARSOVIENNE POSITION — a position borrowed from an old dance of the same name. The lady stands in front of the man, slightly to his right. Both face the same direction. The man holds the lady's right hand in his right hand, and her left hand in his left hand at about shoulder height. The position is infrequently used in ballroom dancing.

KEY TO ABBREVIATIONS

LF, or L .... Left foot
RF, or R .... Right foot
Fwd. .... Forward
Swd. .... Sideward
Bkwd. .... Backward
LOD .... Line of direction
CW .... Clockwise
CCW .... Counterclockwise
Ct(s). .... Count(s)
Meas. .... Measure(s)
Diag. .... Diagonal
Wt. .... Weight
S .... Slow
Q .... Quick

CHAPTER THREE

AUXILIARY DANCES

$\mathbf{M}$any dances fall outside the realm of the traditional ones used in the ballroom. These have unlimited usefulness in a classroom activity devoted to the instruction of beginning dancers. Some serve to take a more permanent place of the short-lived fad dances. Others are useful as tension-relievers, or as icebreakers for getting a class or a party started in a lively manner. The line and circle dances do not involve the use of partners and allow everyone to participate. The auxiliary dances introduce the coordination of easy movement patterns with music which aids the beginning student to understand the same elements as he progresses to dances with more complex structures.

Do not teach the auxiliary dances as an entire unit but intersperse them with the more traditional popular dances.

ZORBA THE GREEK

Motion pictures sometimes inspire a new dance or revive an old one. In "Zorba the Greek," several dances were depicted but the one which fits the theme music is an ancient dance, long popular in Greece, known as Hassapiko. In form, the Hassapiko is similar to many of the antique choral dances found throughout those countries surrounding the eastern Mediterranean which formed the centers of civilization and culture in the Ancient World. Among the names by which these dances are known are Hora, Debka, Oro, and Kolo. Although old in form, the vivacious and carefree spirit of the Hassapiko appeals to contemporary dancers and retains a useful place in the field of popular music.

The theme music for "Zorba the Greek" is in 2/4 time with a

rhythm, or "beat," that is easily distinguished. It is danced "on the beat," and not to the musical phrasing.

Formation: A line, or "chain" of dancers, men and women intermixed in any order, with the leader at the right end of the line. The leader directs his chorus of followers in a general clockwise direction around the dancing area. For the leader to direct effectively, each line should consist of not more than eight or ten dancers. It is considered improper for one leader to pass through the line of another leader.

Dancers hold hands clasped about shoulder high (see illustration), or may be placed with arms out-stretched upon the nearest shoulder of the adjacent dancers. The leader may hold his right hand extended upward and use it to signal changes from the basic pattern, or he may place it upon his right hip.

The leader may begin the dance on *any* accented beat. For this reason all lines may not be performing the same footwork at the same time. Each "chorus" watches its leader for the cue to begin and to direct any variations he may wish to make.

Record: "Zorba the Greek," United Artist #UA-867, Leroy Holmes Orchestra; or other recordings of the same music which employ an even tempo and consistent beat.

Basic Dance Pattern

(All counts are of even duration and follow the accents of the music.)

Steps	Count
Step swd. on RF	1
Cross LF in front of RF and transfer weight upon LF	2
Step swd. on RF	3
Swing LF diag. across to right	4
Step in place on LF	5
Swing RF diag. across to right	6

Repeat as long as desired.

Sliding Variation

(This figure is the same as *chassé* in ballet terminology, and "sashay" in Square dance lingo.)

Steps	Count
Step swd. on RF with sliding step	1
Close LF to RF with sliding step	&

Repeat, continuing to move to the right with quick,
   sliding steps.
Figure may continue as long as leader desires.

Heel-Toe Variation

(Both feet remain close together during the sequence of this variation.)

Steps	Count
With knees bent, pivot on both heels turning toes to right	1
Knees remaining bent, pivot on toes turning heels to right	2

Repeat, pivoting on heels and toes, moving generally to
   the right, as long as leader desires.

In using the variations, the leader calls the changes to his "chorus" or indicates them by some pre-arranged signal with his right hand. Time all transitions smoothly to avoid losing the general rhythm and to keep the line constantly in motion.

SWINGING MIXER

Figures from Square Dancing may be adapted to contemporary music to create a mixer. In mixer dances all the ladies have an opportunity to dance with all the men, and vice versa, for at least a few seconds!

In Swinging Mixer, dancers begin any of the figures with *either foot*. For this reason specific footwork is not given — the dancers follow the rhythm of the music and the fun and enthusiasm generated is more important than exacting technique.

Formation: Partners in a large circle, hands joined all around the circle and all facing the center; lady on man's right.

Record: "Let's Go" (8 count introduction), Colton #BLP-2024, The Ventures; or any other rock 'n roll music which is broken into phrases of eight distinct counts. The dance phrasing corresponds to that of the music.

Dance Pattern

Steps	*Count*
All walk fwd. 4 steps toward center	1, 2, 3, 4
Clap own hands twice against knees, bending fwd.	5, 6
Clap hands twice in front of self	7, 8
All walk bkwd. 4 steps from center	1, 2, 3, 4
Clap own hands twice against knees, bending fwd.	5, 6
Clap hands twice in front of self	7, 8

Swing the corner lady   1 thru 8

(Man turns to girl on his *left*. They take a modified ballroom position in which their right sides are adjacent. With 8 short, quick walking steps turn in place, revolving CW.)

Promenade   1 thru 8

(At the end of Swinging figure, man turns lady so both are facing CCW line of direction; lady on man's right side, inside hands joined. Both take 8 walking steps fwd.)

Repeat as long as desired, making the change of partners on the "swing the corner lady" figure. By momentarily rejoining hands each time the dancers walk toward center, the circle will retain a round formation.

The Bounce*

The Bounce should have a lot of that quality. It allows the same freedom in individuality and styling expressed by many of the contemporary dances and has the added factor of being a group activity in which more than two dancers may participate. There are two parts to the dance.

Formation: Small circles of not more than 9 or 10 dancers, all facing inward. Partners are not required and men and women may be placed in any intermixed order.

Record: "Shake, Shake, Shake" (8 beat introduction), Dore #749, Instrumental; or any contemporary rock 'n roll music may be used.

Part A

Dancers bend slightly forward as arms swing generally outward and upward. Dancers' spines and arms freely "bounce" in undulating movements growing out of the footwork. Dancers stay generally in place; hands are *not* joined with other dancers.

Dance Pattern

Steps	Count	Verbal Cue
Step flat in place on RF, knee bent	1	Bend-
Straighten knee of right leg by pulling it sharply bkwd. RF stays in place but heel "bounces" off floor.		
Bounce should be carried upward through body	&	Straight,
Step flat in place on LF, knee bent	2	Bend-
Straighten knee by pulling it backward, as described	&	Straight,
Step in place on ball of RF	3	Step,
Step in place on ball of LF	&	Step,
Step flat in place on RF, knee bent	4	Bend-
Straighten knee by pulling it backward, as described	&	Straight.
Reverse sequence beginning on LF	1 thru 4-&	
Repeat sequence beginning on RF	1 thru 4-&	
Reverse sequence beginning on LF	1 thru 4-&	

*Dance created by the author.

Part B

Dancers quickly place hands on shoulders of neighbors and entire circle revolves to the left (CW) for four counts; to the right (CCW) four counts; repeating to the left; then right. Dancer's feet and legs remain in crossed position for full four counts in each direction.

Steps	Count	Verbal Cue
Cross RF over LF, and place weight flat upon RF	1	Flat
Quickly transfer weight to toe of LF, which is behind RF	&	Toe
Step to left on flat of RF, which remains crossed over LF (circle moving CW)	2	Flat
Qunickly transfer weight to toe of LF, which is behind RF	&	Toe
Step to left on flat of RF (continuing to move circle CW)	3	Flat
Quickly transfer weight to toe of LF, which is behind RF	&	Toe
Step to left on flat of RF, halting CW movement of circle	4	Flat
Swing LF across in front to the right and reverse entire figure, circle moving to right (CCW)	4 cts.	As above
Repeat circle moving to left (CW)	4 cts.	As above
Reverse circle moving to right (CCW)	4 cts.	As above

Repeat all, alternating Parts A and B.

NEVER ON SUNDAY

Another dance inspired by a motion picture musical theme is "Never on Sunday." The dance is adapted from one originating on the island of Crete, where it is known as Cretiko Syrto. As with the dance for "Zorba the Greek," it is danced "on the beat" and not to the phrasing of the music. In many areas of the United States, the same steps have been applied to a popular Greek Tango titled "Miserlou," and the dance is frequently known by that name.

Formation: A line of dancers with the leader at the right end of the line. No partners are necessary; men and women may be intermixed in any order. Dancers hold clasped hands shoulder high as the leader directs the lines in winding or spiraling patterns about the hall. A leader should never pass through the line of another leader. Each leader begins when he feels the accent of the music. The followers observe the leader for any change he may wish to make. Short lines of eight or ten dancers cooperate better than longer lines.

Record: "Never On Sunday," United Artists #1602, Don Costa Orchestra; "Never On Sunday," Dolton BLP-2019, The Ventures; and many other recordings of the same theme music.

Basic Pattern

Steps	Count	Rhythm
Step to right on RF, turning body to face toward right end of line	1	S
Cross LF diagonally over right leg and touch toe of LF to floor	2	S
Swing left leg behind right leg and step on LF	3	Q
Step sdwd. (short step) on RF	&	Q
Step on LF in front of right, turning toe to left and pivoting to face left end of line. (Dancer aids pivot by lifting from within middle body to bring weight up on toe of LF).	4	S
Step fwd. (toward left end of line) on RF	5	Q
Take short step fwd. (toward left end of line) on LF	&	Q
Step fwd. (toward left end of line) on RF, lifting from middle body to rise on toe of RF	6	S
(Remain facing left end of line for following three steps.)		
Take step bkwd. on LF	7	Q
Take short step bkwd. on RF	&	Q
Step bkwd. on LF, lifting from middle body to pivot toward right end of line in preparation for repeating entire sequence.	8	S

After the students have become thoroughly acquainted with the basic pattern, they may enjoy experimenting with some variations. The leader should be able to clearly indicate, either vocally or by a signal, any variations he wishes to use.

Two variations are notated in which the changes occur in the middle of the basic pattern; the beginning and ending figures remain the same as the basic sequence. Because the variations require more beats to perform, the count will also vary from that given for the basic pattern. Students may also devise other changes in the basic form if they desire.

Single-Cross Variation

Steps	Count	Rhythm
Counts 1 thru 4 remain the same as in the basic pattern with the exception that dancers do not make a complete turn to face left end of line but turn only enough to face front	1 thru 4	As Basic
Swing RF across in front of left leg to bring RF down beside LF (*Outside* of feet are touching, ankles tightly crossed)	5	S
Swing LF around in front of right leg to bring LF down beside RF (Feet and ankles reverse of ct. 5)	6	S
Swing RF around in front of left leg to bring RF down beside LF (Feet and ankles as in ct. 5)	7	S
(Counts 5, 6, 7 may remain in place or may progress fwd. a few inches.)		
End the sequence with cts. 7-&, 8 of the basic pattern, which have become	8-&, 9	Q-Q, S
(Dancers turn on new count of 8 to face left end of line.)		

Triple-Cross Variation

Counts 1 through 4 remain the same as in the basic pattern with the exception that dancers face front as in the Single-Cross Variation.

Steps	Count	Rhythm
Swing RF across in front of left leg to take long step swd. on RF	5	S

With legs remaining in crossed position, close LF beside RF, transferring weight to LF	&	Q
With legs remaining crossed, take short step swd. to left on RF	6	Q

(Entire figure moves swd. to left.)

Reverse cts. 5, &-6 to move figure swd. to right. Begin by swinging LF across to take long step to right	7, &-8	S, Q-Q
Repeat cts. 5, &-6, moving swd. to left	9, &-10	S, Q-Q
End sequence with same steps as cts. 7-&, 8 of basic pattern, which have become	11-&, 12	Q-Q, S

SAN FRANCISCO STOMP*

A contemporary dance in which the dancers express their own individuality and styling. Knees and bodies should be relaxed to permit freedom of movement with a vital, "springy," action. Footwork is generally flat with an earthy quality.

While all counts of the dance are of even duration, the illusion of a syncopated rhythm is created by the use of tapped-clapped accents at irregular intervals.

* Dance created by the author.

Formation: Any number of dancers, without partners, in lines across dancing area. All face a common front. Dancers remain in place for entire sequence, moving slightly from side to side as they dance. Arms move freely with dancer's body rhythm.

Record: "Walk Right In," Vanguard #VRS-35017, Rooftop Singers; "Walk Right In," Dolton #BLP-2024, The Ventures; "Alley Cat," Roper #152, Roper Orchestra; "Washington Square," Epic #5-2224, Village Stompers; or any moderate tempo rock 'n roll music with a well-marked two-beat rhythm.

(Unless there is a definite introduction for the selected music, the dance may begin on *any* accented beat, but with all dancers starting together. The 20-beat pattern of the dance sequence does *not* follow the musical phrasing. Each of the 20 counts of the dance pattern is of the same duration and should be "on the beat.")

Dance Pattern

Steps	Count
Step swd. on RF	1
Step in back of RF on LF	2
Step swd. on RF	3
Tap LF beside RF, at same time, clap hands	4
(Reverse first sequence) Step swd. on LF	5
Step in back of LF on RF	6
Step swd. on LF	7
Tap RF beside LF, at same time, clap hands	8
(Repeat first sequence) Step swd. on RF	9
Step in back of RF on LF	10
Step swd. on RF	11
Tap LF beside RF, at same time, clap hands	12
Step in place on LF, at same time, kick RF fwd.	13
Step in place on RF, at same time, kick LF fwd.	14
Step swd. on LF	15
Tap RF beside LF, at same time, clap hands	16
Step swd. on RF	17
Tap LF beside RF, at same time, clap hands	18
Step swd. on LF, pivoting in place ¼ turn to right (CW)	19
Tap RF beside LF, at same time, clap hands	20

Dance repeats from beginning with all dancers facing a new direction. The changes of direction can be clarified by using the four walls of the room as focal points. It will take four sequences to make the turn of the "square" to again face the original wall. The quarter-turn is *always* made on the *19th* count.

CHAPTER FOUR

CHA-CHA

BACKGROUND "Cha-Cha" is the name of the dance; cha-cha-cha is the figure characteristic to the dance which gives it its name!

The Cha-Cha derives from a rhythmically complex Cuban dance, the Mambo. The Mambo in turn had originated by adding a syncopated, or "jazz," beat to one of the Cuban rhythms which we know as the Rumba. Because Mambo was danced entirely to the offbeat it proved to be extremely difficult for dancers in the United States who were not accustomed to the subtle undercurrent of rhythm created by unfamiliar Afro-Cuban instruments. Dance orchestras also found the music difficult to master.

Most of the figures in the Mambo were of an improvizational nature which depended upon the skill of the performers. One figure popular with most Mambo dancers was called the "Chatch" because it included a triple shuffle of the feet that made a "cha-cha-cha" sound. In the early 1950's, this figure became a complete dance by itself. The new Cha-Cha was no longer danced to the offbeat and dance orchestras modified the musical rhythm to a basic count of *slow, slow, quick-quick, slow.*

Many of the South American and Caribbean countries claim to be the originators of Cha-Cha, but most dance historians are inclined to believe it owes its true origin to ardent adherents of Afro-Latin music and dance in the New York City area. Whatever its exact origin, the Cha-Cha definitely retains and displays the spirit and rhythm of a true Latin-American dance.

STYLING "Like a chicken digging for worms" was one description given to Cha-Cha when it was first displayed to the public.

53

This reference was to the earthy, flat-footed manner of "digging" the feet into the floor on the slow counts of the music. While this style has become modified and softened over a period of years, the feet are still placed flatly upon the floor without the gliding or sliding movement that is found in dances such as the Tango, or Waltz. The feet remain close to the floor, and are picked up and put down with a slight knee action. As in most Latin-American dances, the hips are also kept relaxed so there is a freedom of movement in the pelvic section. Generally, the upper body moves over the supporting foot as a step is taken forward, backward, or to the side. In challenge position, where the arms are free, they move naturally in relation to the rhythm of the body without being forced into artificial patterns. When closed ballroom position is used in Cha-Cha, the dance is more restricted in styling and body movement. In ballroom position the lady does not have an opportunity to improvise but must mirror the steps and styling indicated by the man.

For beginning dancers the open challenge position is usually the better of the two. It helps to eliminate the beginner's fear of "making a mistake" which often can become inhibiting. While both dancers must follow the rhythm established by the music they may each follow their own stylings and patterns of movement. At the same time they must strive to create a unified rapport between each other so that they dance as one unit and not as two soloists. Cha-Cha may be danced in either an exaggerated form or a more conservative manner, so encourage beginning students to try both.

Cha-Cha is essentially a "spot" dance. This means that it is danced in a small area without progressing around the room as does the Foxtrot, or the Waltz. For this reason, dancers should always have enough area around them to dance without being inhibited by the close proximity of other couples.

RHYTHM ANALYSIS   Cha-Cha is played in 4/4 time, which means that there are four beats to the measure. The third beat is cut into two quick counts, creating a rhythm of slow, slow, quick-quick, slow. A graphic diagram of two measures looks like this:

4/4	○	○	⬩	○	○	○	⬩	○
Count	1	2	3-&	4	1	2	3-&	4
Rhythm	S	S	Q-Q	S	S	S	Q-Q	S
Steps	L	R	L-R	L	R	L	R-L	R

Note that the footwork alternates with each measure, that is, if the dancer begins with the left foot on one measure, the following measure begins on the right foot.

Cha-Cha is danced "on the beat," that is, the footwork must coincide with the basic rhythm of the music.

The instructor will find it a helpful aid in rhythm recognition to mark the rhythm with Claves, or other instruments typical to Latin-American music (see section on EAR TRAINING).

TEACHING PROGRESSIONS   While listening to several Cha-Cha recordings of different tempos, students may indicate their knowledge of the rhythm by clapping hands, or snapping fingers. When they have learned to hear and follow the basic rhythm it is time for them to turn the rhythm into physical action with their feet and bodies.

Place the students in the dancing area so that each one has sufficient room to move freely. At this point students should work without partners and with little regard to styling. The instructor should be located in a position easy for all students to see and hear. Without music, but marking the rhythm by either counting or by using a simple percussion instrument, have the students walk through the series of following exercises, both men and women following the same footwork:

Marking Time In Place

	Count	Rhythm
Step in place on LF	1	S
Step in place on RF	2	S
Step in place on LF	3	Q
Step in place on RF	&	Q
Step in place on LF	4	S

Reverse figure beginning with RF on ct. 1. The rhythm may also be counted *step, step, cha-cha-cha*. Repeat this figure several times, counting it by different methods.

Forward and Backward

	Count	Rhythm
Step fwd. on LF	1	S
Step fwd. on RF	2	S
Step fwd. on LF	3	Q
Step fwd. on RF	&	Q
Step fwd. on LF	4	S

Reverse all, moving *backward* beginning with RF. Repeat several times, using different manners of counting.

Front Diagonal Crossover

	Count	Rhythm
Step diagonally fwd. toward right on LF	1	S
Step back in place on RF	2	S
Step in place on LF	3	Q
Step in place on RF	&	Q
Step in place on LF	4	S

Reverse all, stepping diagonally across to left with RF on ct. 1. Repeat exercise several times.

Back Diagonal Crossover

This figure is similar to the Front Diagonal Crossover, except that the cross is made to the rear.

	Count	Rhythm
Step diagonally backward to right on LF	1	S
Step fwd. in place on RF	2	S
Step in place on LF	3	Q
Step in place on RF	&	Q
Step in place on LF	4	S

Reverse by leading back with RF on ct. 1. Repeat with various counting methods.

Turns On Slow Counts

	Count	Rhythm
Beginning with LF, step out to left side with toe of LF leading a small turn to left	1	S

Continue turn moving to left by bringing RF
    across and transferring weight on RF   2   S
Cha-cha-cha, LF-RF-LF, figure in place   3-& Q-Q S
Reverse all, making turn to right.

In the initial exercises the degree of turn made on the two slow counts is not important. In subsequent lessons this figure may be developed into a half-turn or a full-turn. The footwork remains essentially the same but the degree of turn is controlled by the amount of "push" supplied by the shoulders and upper body of the dancer. In the turns, the instructor should observe that counts 1 and 2 receive an equal amount of time. Otherwise the turns will develop an unevenness that tends to throw the dancers off balance. Repeat exercise until it is performed with ease.

Turns On Cha-Cha-Cha

	Count	Rhythm
Step in place on RF	1	S
Step in place on LF	2	S
Begin turn to left by stepping to left on LF with toe turned to left	3	Q
Continue turning to left by bringing RF across to left and transferring weight to RF	&	Q
Step in place on LF	4	S

Reverse all, turning to right on cts. 3-&. Repeat exercise.

The objective of the above series of exercises is to demonstrate that an easy combination of footwork may be made to look and even feel entirely different by the expedient method of changing the direction of some of the steps without altering the basic change-of-weight structure. This truth may also be applied to dances other than Cha-Cha.

When the dancers have gained this much knowledge of co-ordinating footwork and rhythm, they are ready to work on the styling of the dance. Encourage individual styling as long as it conforms to the earthy, relaxed character that has come to be associated with Cha-Cha. An easy figure to use in developing styling is one known as the Rock, or Rocking, figure. Most dance authorities consider it the basic, or foundation figure in Cha-

Cha. It uses the same footwork and rhythm followed in the previous exercises. While initially learning the figure, both men and women may begin with the same foot, and both should still be working without partners.

Basic Rock, Forward

	Count	Rhythm
Take short step fwd. on LF, stepping flat on ball of foot with left knee slightly bent. Let weight of entire upper body move over LF. (RF remains in original place but without weight upon it.)	1	S
Step back in place on RF, shifting entire weight of body over RF. (In the shifting of the body weight fwd. or back, there should be a feeling of resistance, similar to that experienced in the same movements in a swimming pool. The shoulders and arms are relaxed and move in rhythmic coordination with the body.)	2	S
Step in place on LF	3	Q
Step in place on RF	&	Q
Step in place on LF	4	S

Basic Rock, Backward

This figure is the exact counterpart of the Forward Rock. It begins by taking a short step back on RF, shifting entire weight backward over RF, etc.

Care must be taken not to let the cha-cha-cha figure (cts. 3-&, 4) develop into stamping steps. Later, when the students have learned the use of the Triplet figure (see TERMINOLOGY), these counts may be developed into ones which move slightly forward or backward, rather than in place.

To a verbal or to a percussion rhythm, repeat the Basic Rock figures, forward and back, a few times to observe the styling as well as the timing. When the students are familiar with the figure let them dance it to a recording that has a well-marked rhythm. Apply the same styling to some of the other figures which have been previously explored and practice them to music. Observe that they do not become so involved with footwork patterns as to ignore the rhythm established by the music. A selection of several Cha-Cha recordings helps the students in learning to listen for the basic rhythm in a variety of orchestrations.

When sufficient confidence and coordination have been gained it is time to begin working with partners. For this, the most comfortable position is the challenge position with hands joined straight across, the man holds the woman's right hand in his left hand, and her left hand in his right hand (see section on POSITIONS). In this position the woman performs the counterpart of the man's steps.

To assure a strong lead and response, both partners need to keep a little tension in their arms. As the man steps forward with his left foot he pushes with his left hand so that the woman knows to step back with her right foot. The reverse is true as the man steps backward; he pulls, or leads, his partner toward him so that she steps forward.

For the initial experience of a man and woman dancing together in the Cha-Cha, use the Basic Rock figure in challenge position with hands held directly across. The instructor may cue the lead for the man in this manner:

Forward Rock

	Count	Rhythm	Foot
Push with left hand	1	S	L
Pull with right hand	2	S	R
Cha-cha-cha (as both partners presumably know the basic sequence, a strong lead is not necessary on this part.)	3-& 4	Q-Q S	L-R L

Back Rock

	Count	Rhythm	Foot
Pull with right hand	1	S	R
Push with left hand	2	S	L
Cha-cha-cha	3-& 4	Q-Q S	R-L R

Encourage the men to exaggerate their lead in the beginning. This can always be smoothed down and made more subtle as both men and women develop skill and confidence.

Practice the Basic Rock figure to music, observing that the men are leading and the women responding. Also be certain that the dancers stay "with the beat."

Next, try the Forward and Backward figure as a couple figure. For this, the man moves forward for five steps in the basic rhythm as he leads the lady to move backwards. Reverse the steps so that the man is leading backward and the lady forward.

The Front Diagonal Crossover is more complex, but should not offer too great a challenge to the dancers. On the first count the man leads the lady so that she steps diagonally across in front of herself with her RF as he does the same with his LF. The diagonal cross figure continues with the same footwork which was practiced without partners. To make the turn freer, dancers usually find it more comfortable to drop the hold of the hands toward which they are turning. Hands are quickly rejoined during the last part of the cha-cha-cha figure so that the man may then lead the figure diagonally across in the opposite direction.

Repeat some of the other figures which were explored without partners, but with the lady dancing the exact counterpart of the man's steps.

As a practice device, the instructor may make a simple sequence of three or four patterns, using four or six measures for each pattern. This will assist in developing a sense of changing the lead for the men while the ladies learn to respond to the change.

As soon as possible, students should begin making their own sequence of figures. When a practice sequence is used the students must be made to realize that it is a teaching device and they should be urged to break away from a set pattern as soon as they are ready. For the first few measures of Cha-Cha, it is wise to adhere to the hands-across challenge position. This allows the partners to establish the "feel of the rhythm" in common. When this has been established partners may then drop the hand hold and are free to improvise their own sequence of footwork. They may return to the hand hold position as frequently as they desire. Cha-Cha should be as free-moving as possible with partners dancing around one another as well as back and forth in place. The instructor should inspire the stu-

dents to respond to the music rather than to dance to a memorized sequence of movements.

In subsequent sessions, after the students have learned some
of the other dances, they will enjoy adding additional figures to
their Cha-Cha repertory, such as the following:

Side Break

Perform this in either closed or challenge position. Directions
are for man, woman does counterpart.

	Count	Rhythm
Step swd. to left on LF, without turning toe out, but bending knee slightly. Let full body weight move swd. over LF	1	S
Step swd. to right with RF, pulling full weight over RF to regain upright position	2	S
Cha-cha-cha, LF-RF-LF, in place	3-& 4	Q-Q S

This figure may be cued verbally: "Fall, recover, cha-cha-cha."
Repeat figure "falling" to right side.

The Chase

The Chase is a figure for fun, but without sufficient experience and confidence many students find it confusing. The turn
at the beginning of the figure seems to be the stumbling block.
Many believe that this must be executed by some exacting
method rather than being a free-style turn. To overcome this
inhibiting factor, the instructor stresses that *any* turn, in *any*
direction, beginning with *either* foot, is permissible as long as
it is performed naturally and "on the beat."

The Chase may develop from any figure in which the dancers
are face-to-face, either in closed or challenge position.

	Count	Rhythm
The man begins the figure by making a sharp turn away from his partner (*either* foot, *either* direction)	1	S
Man continues to move fwd. in direction away from woman	2	S
(Woman marks time in place on these initial 2 counts.)		

Man continues traveling away from woman on
  cha-cha-cha steps   3-&4 Q-Q S
(On the same cha-cha-cha figure, the woman moves forward
  to end closely behind man, that is, she "chases" him.)

On the repeat of the sequence, both make a sharp turn (any
type) to move back in the opposite line of direction. The woman
is then leading away and the man is "chasing" her. The figure
continues to repeat until one partner tires of the figure and does
not make the turn. When the other partner discovers that he or
she is again facing his or her partner, the "chase" is over and
they go into another figure.

The Chase may develop into a game of "tag" in which the
person in the rear tags the one in front on the shoulder (ct. 4);
or the dancer in the rear may place both hands on the hips of
the leading partner. Frequently, several couples join into a long
line for this, or other, variations of The Chase.

While younger people prefer the freedom of the challenge
position in Cha-Cha, they should occasionally be requested to
dance it in ballroom position. This position requires a stronger
lead on the part of the man and serves as a good checking device
of his leading ability, or lack of it.

CHAPTER FIVE

ARGENTINE TANGO

BACKGROUND   The fact that *two* dances termed the Tango exist
has compounded confusion among both dancers and musicians
for many years. The two have very little in common other than
the name.

The original dance to carry the name comes from Spain. The
Spanish Tango is a staccato dance, written in 2/4 tempo, somewhat resembling a Habanera rhythm. The Spanish Tango is *not*
a ballroom type of dance but is an *exhibition* dance performed
as a *solo*. It blends the Flamenco and Classical Spanish dance
forms, accented by sharp heel rhythms, snapping fingers, and
contrasting arm movements which flow in soft counter patterns.
The Spanish Tango is performed in a small dancing area, often
atop a small table.

The *Argentine Tango* is a *couple* dance performed in closed
position with progressive movements directed around the room.
The music of the Argentine Tango is written in a sustained,
moderately slow 4/4 tempo. The exact origin of the Argentine
Tango is credited to the Gauchos, the sturdy cowboys of the
Argentine pampas, who sought relaxation by dancing with the
Senoritas in the bistros of Buenos Aires. Historians date the beginning of the Argentine Tango at about 1880, but both the
music and the dance have undergone extensive modifications
since that time.

Other dances popular during the formative years of the
Argentine Tango were the *Viennese Waltz, Polka, Mazurka,
Habanera, Verbena,* and the *Milonga.* All of them had some influence in forming the character of the new dance, as did the folk
dances of Spain, the native homeland of many of the Gauchos.

In Argentina, the dance was originally termed *el baile con
corté* – the "dance with a stop." When or why it finally became
known as the "Tango," the same name as its distant Spanish

cousin, is difficult to trace, but the change probably occurred when the dance was taken to France and exhibited in a sensationalized form before the novelty-seeking Parisians. The Tango was first introduced to dancers in the United States in about 1913, when the leading exhibition dancers of that era performed it.

For beginning dancers, the less complicated figures of the Argentine Tango are ideal to use as the first closed position dance for several reasons: (a) the dance is sufficiently slow for the beginning dancer to coordinate easily the movement with the music while learning to lead or follow simple figures; (b) the steps resemble normal walking steps more closely than those in other dances; (c) the music is well marked and easy to hear; (d) the simple variations that can be built upon the basic rhythm hold the interest of those students who may have had experience with other dances; (e) the romantic connotation of the Argentine Tango provides sustaining interest in learning the dance.

STYLING   In its travels through the Argentine, France, England, and the United States, the Tango has developed different styles, apparent mostly in the positioning of the body, but not radically different in the fundamental step combinations. In the United States, dancers use the erect posture position, with neither partner leaning upon the other for support. Although the typical change of rhythm from slow to quick creates a dynamic change, the change must be made smoothly without any obvious bounce or unevenness. In the slow movements, the dancers need to learn to sustain the movement to maintain a body "aliveness" between steps. Generally, all steps originate from the hips, and not below the knees. The feet must remain close to the floor in smooth, gliding movements with no evidence of picking-up and putting-down of the feet. The most desirable type of movement in the Tango, but one which requires practice, is a "heavy-light" cat-like tread, without bouncing or syncopated movements in the knees or upper body. Each time the dancer takes a step he moves his upper body over the standing foot. The characteristic Tango style of movement developed from the clothing worn by the original dancers of the Argentine Tango — the ladies gowned in long, heavily ruffled skirts; the Gauchos in thick, bulky trousers and with heavy leather boots fitted with large metal spurs.

RHYTHM ANALYSIS   The Argentine Tango has a heavily accented musical beat that is easily heard and "felt" by most dancers. The musical phrase and the dance pattern phrase coincide. The student needs to learn to recognize the musical phrasing as well as the pulsating beat. The musical phrases are written in two-measure units of 4/4 time, which makes an underlying rhythm of eight slow beats. A graphic diagram of the two-measure unit looks like this:

4/4	◯	◯	◯	◯	◯	◯	◯	◯
Count	1	2	3	4	5	6	7	8
Rhythm	S	S	S	S	S	S	S	S
Steps	L	R	L	R	L	R	L	R

TEACHING PROGRESSIONS   Gather the students around the phonograph to listen and become familiar with the music and to learn to hear both the underlying beat of the music and the musical phrasing. It will be necessary for them to learn to distinguish the count of 1 in the phrasing. After the instructor has explained the rhythm and phrasing, the students mark the rhythm by counting aloud, clapping lightly, or snapping their fingers.

When the students understand the rhythm sufficiently, direct them to go out on the floor to practice coordinating the footwork with the rhythm. Without partners, and moving in a counter-clockwise direction around the floor, walk in rhythm counting beats 1 through 8, taking one step on each beat of music. Use normal walking steps without injecting correct dance styling until after the students are able to coordinate movement and rhythm. The instructor may use the directional call, "slow, slow, slow," in counting. Repeat the exercise by having all students begin with the *left* foot, as the instructor counts, in rhythm, "left, right, left, right." Keep to the usual counter-clockwise line of direction but observe that the students do not inhibit their movements by following one another in a single file.

Repeat the exercise with all students moving backwards.

Alternate eight counts forward with eight counts backward.

Repeat briefly, using four counts forward and four counts backward.

Explain the dance-walk to the students and repeat the above exercises briefly, still without using partners, paying attention to the toe lead as they take forward or backward steps. Take moderately long steps, but in an effortless and natural fashion. The movement of each leg originates from the hip. Each dancer needs to lift the middle body slightly to sustain a continuity of movement with a sense of "aliveness" in the body.

After the instructor analyzes and demonstrates leading and following, the students may take partners to repeat some of the exercises which they previously practiced alone. Do not stress correct styling until *after* the students gain some experience in working with a partner in closed position. For a short time, use only the *slow* steps, but encourage the students to experiment with simple changes in direction by moving in small circles or in zig-zag patterns, or others. The ladies use footwork counter to that used by the men.

After practicing the coordinating of the *slow* counts of the music with *slow* steps in the footwork, the students will be able to meet the challenge of combining *slow* and *quick* rhythms.

The figure generally considered to be the foundation pattern of the Tango is called either the Tango March, or more frequently, the "basic" Tango figure. In the basic combinations, the third and seventh *slow* beats are cut into two *quick* beats, producing a "slow, slow, quick-quick, slow," rhythm in each measure, as illustrated in the graphic diagram:

4/4								
Count	1	2	3-&	4	5	6	7-&	8
Rhythm	S	S	Q-Q	S	S	S	Q-Q	S
Steps	L	R	L-R	L	R	L	R-L	R

Bring to the students' attention the fact that the footwork alternates with each measure; if the dancer begins with the *left* foot on the count of *1*, then he steps on the *right* foot on count 5, the beginning of the second measure, or in the reverse order.

Briefly repeat some of the former exercises using the newly introduced "basic" rhythm. If the students have enough skill let them continue to practice with partners. For the benefit of the men, demonstrate the necessity of using their hands to communicate to their partners the change of steps. Also demonstrate that the size of the *quick* steps follows the same relative pattern established in dividing the music; the *quick* steps are proportionately shorter than the *long* steps taken on the *slow* counts.

Using the "slow, slow, quick-quick, slow" rhythm, explore simple changes in direction to achiéve the effect of inventing a "new" figure without altering the basic footwork. Explore circular, zig-zag, and movements from side to side.

When the students have become comfortably familiar with the Tango March, or "basic" pattern, make a slight change to incorporate the Corté, or "stop," as part of the eight-count dance

phrase. The Corté takes two slow counts and may be interjected at any place in the dance, but for simplicity's sake use it as the first two counts of the Tango March pattern.

Perform Corté in closed position. The man steps backward on his left foot; the *left* knee slightly bent and the foot turned out to the left (see illustration). The turn-out of foot serves as a brake to hold the foot in place and to assure a strong balance. The man's upper body remains erect as it moves backward over the left foot. The man's *right* foot stays in place on the floor, slightly ahead of the standing foot, but with no weight upon it.

The lady does the exact counterpart, stepping forward onto her *right* foot, while keeping the *left* foot pointed toward the floor. She supports her own weight without falling forward upon the man (see illustration).

For both dancers, the transition of weight from one foot to the other must be smoothly controlled without either partner pulling the other off balance. Use the entire "slow" count to make the "dip."

On the second "slow" count, the man steps forward transferring his weight onto his right foot to recover an upright position. The lady does the counterpart. The Tango March, or "basic" figure, then continues from the 3rd count, or, "quick-quick, slow; slow, slow, quick-quick, slow."

The change of direction in the Corté seems awkward at first to the majority of the students, but this disappears after repeating the entire figure several times. Present the Corté-March combination as the first figure in the practice routine.

Although the Argentine Tango has more patterns than any other dance, we have chosen to discuss only four typical figures as a practice sequence. Practice each figure separately before combining it with another. Do not lead students to believe that the practice sequence is the only possible combination of the figures given. Each figure of eight counts is *one unit* which the students eventually will be able to *rearrange in any order* of their preference. After the students have developed some proficiency with the practice routine they may add more figures.

Practice Routine — Argentine Tango
(Description is for the man; lady dances exact counterpart.)

FIGURE I — CORTÉ AND MARCH. (Figure moves in LOD)

		Count	Rhythm
Meas. 1	Step bkwd. on LF, knee slightly bent	1	S
	Step fwd. on RF, recovering upright posture	2	S
	Step fwd. on LF, then on RF	3 &	Q-Q
	Step fwd. on LF	4	S
Meas. 2	Step fwd. on RF	5	S
	Step fwd. on LF	6	S
	Step fwd. on RF, then on LF	7 &	Q-Q
	Step fwd. on RF	8	S

FIGURE II — BOX AND SIDE DRAW. (Figure remains in place.)

		Count	Rhythm
Meas. 1	Step fwd. on LF	1	S
	Step swd. on RF	&	Q
	Close LF beside RF (changing weight)	2	Q
	Step bkwd. on RF	3	S
	Step swd. on LF	&	Q
	Close RF beside LF (changing weight)	4	Q

(Note: The above four cts. form a "box," or "square," pattern.)

		Count	Rhythm
	Take a *long* step swd. to left with LF	5	S
	Draw RF to arch of LF *without* transferring weight	6	S
	Take a *long* step swd. to right with RF	7	S
	Draw LF to arch of RF *without* transferring weight	8	S

FIGURE III — DIAGONAL MARCH — PROMENADE POSITION. (Figure moves on *shallow* diagonals while progressing generally fwd. in LOD.)

		Count	Rhythm
Meas. 1	In promenade position, turn *slightly* toward center. Step fwd. on LF	1	S

	Count	Rhythm
Continue on diag., step fwd on RF	2	S
Step fwd. on LF	3	Q
Step fwd. on RF	&	Q
Step fwd. on LF (man drawing lady into closed position)	4	S

Meas. 2   In reverse promenade position, turn *slightly* away from center. (Note: Lady will be on man's left. Maintain ballroom hold, but adjust arm positions for comfort.)

	Count	Rhythm
Step fwd. on RF	5	S
Step fwd. on LF, continuing outward diag.	6	S
Step fwd. on RF	7	Q
Step fwd. on LF	&	Q
Step fwd. on RF (man drawing lady into closed position)	8	S

FIGURE IV — SCISSORS. (Figure is danced in place, with side to side movement.)

	Count	Rhythm
Meas. 1 Open into promenade position, facing center, step fwd. on LF	1	S
Step fwd. on RF (toward center)	2	S
Step on LF, turning to closed position	3	Q
Step swd. on RF, facing partner	&	Q
Step across in front of self to right side with LF	4	S
Meas. 2 Step swd. to right with RF	5	Q
Step swd. on LF, facing partner	&	Q
Step across in front of self to left side with RF (lady also crosses *in front* of self)	6	S

(Note: On cts. 3 through 6, partners remain facing, shifting weight from side to side with a balancing motion. The crossing of the feet gives the figure the "Scissors" title. The action may be cued: "balance, balance, cross.")

	Count	Rhythm
Take long step fwd. on LF	7	Q
Step swd. to right on RF	&	Q

Draw LF to arch of RF without chang-
ing weight   8   S
(Note: Cts. 7 & 8 are termed the "Tango
Close" combination, frequently used at the
end of a phrase. The action may be cued:
"forward, side, arch.")

After the students can execute the practice routine, encourage
them to rearrange the four figures in any order of their choice.
If necessary, review all figures individually.

If the teaching schedule permits, students may enjoy adding
the following two figures to their Tango repertory.

SWINGOVER COMBINATION. (Figure progresses fwd. in LOD as
    lady moves across from side to side.)

		Count	Rhythm
Meas. 1	In open position, man's right arm be-hind lady's back, step fwd. on LF	1	S
	Step fwd. on RF	2	S
	Man continues fwd. with short steps, LF, RF, LF	3 & 4	Q-Q S

(On same counts, man leads lady across in
front of himself, moving her from his right side
to his left side. Lady steps RF (Q), LF (Q),
RF (S), momentarily facing man as she steps
across.)

Meas. 2	In open position, man's left arm be-hind lady's back, step fwd. on RF	5	S
	Step fwd. on LF	6	S
	Man continues fwd. with short steps, RF, LF, RF	7 & 8	Q-Q S

(On same counts, man uses left arm to lead
lady back to his right side. Lady again momentarily faces man as she steps across, LF
(Q), RF (Q), LF (S).)

The dancers may repeat the *Swingover Combination* to form
a 16 count sequence.

DIP AND TURN COMBINATION. (Figure begins moving forward in
    LOD, then against LOD.)

		Count	Rhythm
Meas. 1	In promenade position, step fwd. on LF	1	S
	Step fwd. on RF	2	S
	Step fwd. on LF	3	Q
	Step fwd. on RF	&	Q
	Step fwd. on LF, bending left knee into a "dip," or forward Corté position. Retain promenade position.	4	S
Meas. 2	Step bkwd. on RF, partially turning inward toward partner	5	S
	Step on LF toward partner to complete half turn facing against LOD	6	S
	Make individual turn in place, releasing hand holds. Man turns to right, CW, stepping RF (Q), LF (Q). (Lady turns to left, CCW, stepping LF (Q), RF (Q).)	7 &	Q-Q
	Step on RF beside partner, resuming closed position facing LOD	8	Q
	Draw LF to arch of RF, without transferring weight	&	Q

(Note: The *Dip* and *Turn* combination may be further enhanced by using the first 2 counts for a Corté, as in Fig. I. An underarm turn may also be used on the same counts. In the underarm turn, the man leads the lady under their clasped arms; his left, her right. The lady turns outward to her right, stepping RF (S), LF (S) progressing slightly fwd. in LOD, making a half turn on each step to end in closed position. Man travels fwd. in LOD, stepping LF (S), RF (S), adjusting the length of his steps to control the lady's turn.)

With the understanding of the Argentine Tango the students have gained through the practice figures, prompt them to make combinations of their own. By exploring creative combinations of slow and quick steps within the basic 8-count framework, and by employing turns, changes of direction, or other devices, students can create ingenious patterns. Students remember and dance their own figures long after the practice combinations have been forgotten.

CHAPTER SIX

AMERICAN WALTZ

BACKGROUND "Create a dance in waltz rhythm that is too complicated for those blundering peasants to perform!" This, supposedly, was the command issued by one of the imperious princes of the Hapsburg aristocracy to his court choreographers.

Vienna, as well as all of Europe, had been dominated for more than a century by the stilted court charades which emanated from the regal palaces of France. Elaborately contrived minuets and contra dances were created by trained choreographers and danced at lavish balls over which haughty masters of ceremony presided. The dancers, frequently robed in costly masquerade costumes, moved through exacting formations with affected courtesies and feigned fervor. Although many of the court dances were adapted from folk dances of many nations, they were completely drained of all the power, spontaneity, and earthiness of the original. All that remained was a hollow imitation which had been polished to an artful luster. They could be performed only by dancers fortunate enough to be able to study the intricate and exacting figures under the guidance of dancing masters.

Early stirrings of rebellion by the people of France also reawakened a resurgance of national art and culture among the people of neighboring countries. In Austria, dances in 3/4 time had existed among the peasant population from as far back as the middle ages. These dances were popular at weddings, christenings, and harvest festivals and were danced to old tunes known as *Ländla*, literally signifying Upper Austria and Steiermark. The dances, characterized by fast turning figures in which the women were frequently lifted off their feet by the men who

marked the rhythm with their heavy, hob-nailed boots, eventually became known as *Ländlers*. The Ländler, using the old
step pattern of step-close-step, is still danced in many of the
rural areas of Austria, Germany, Switzerland, and Hungary.

As Austria became the focal point of European musical and
literary culture, the interest in her native dances also increased.
The Ländler was moved from the rural areas into the drawing
rooms of the elite. The transition from hob-nailed boots to thin-
soled dancing slippers, and the use of polished hardwood dancing floors in place of rough planks or packed-earth dancing areas
brought a marked change in the character of the dance. Instead
of being a leaping, stamping dance, it became one in which
turning and gliding was the distinctive trait. The German word
Walzer, sigifying "sliding or gliding" was first applied to the
new form of the dance in about 1760.

As the French Revolution came to an end, so did the highly
synthetic French court culture which had dominated European
social life for so long. In Austria, the new Walzer came to be
danced more and more frequently. It signified a release from
the restrictions of the old order to the freedom of the new. At
court functions and in the fashionable salons dancers were able
for the first time to choose their own partners and to move freely
around the ballroom in their own pattern of turning and gliding
figures.

Another important change did take place in the Walzer, however. Whether it resulted from some legendary prince ordering
his court choreographers to "make the dance too complicated for
the peasants," or whether it was a normal process of evolution
that brought the change can only be conjectured.

In the period closely following the French Rebellion the step
pattern used in the old Ländler of *step-close-step*, which brought
the feet together on the *second* count of the music, became
changed to *step-side-close*. In the new footwork, the feet were
brought together on the *third* beat of the music. In addition,
the position of holding partners face-to-face for the entire dance
became characteristic. In the Ländler, the closed position had
been occasionally inserted into the dance for short intervals of
two or three measures.

The new footwork, while more complex, seemed to stimulate rather than deter interest in learning the new form. Shopgirls, chambermaids, messenger boys, and greengrocers were caught up in the excitement of the new waltz and were able to master the skill and dexterity required to perform the fast, whirling turns in a smooth and graceful manner. All strata of Austrian society ultimately succumbed to the freedom of the dance, and government leaders frankly admitted they would rather waltz than attend to the dull tasks of statesmanship.

The new dance prompted both civic and church officials to voice forceful objections to the intimacy of the face-to-face position. In many areas authorities banned the dance and numerous articles condemning it were published throughout Europe. The overwhelming popularity of the dance eventually overcame the protests and the restrictions placed upon it. The closed position became the standard one for ballroom dancing and has been used in the majority of dances developed since that era.

In Vienna, as the popularity increased, so did the tempo with which the music was played. Johann Strauss, Jr., (1825-1899), who succeeded his father as "Waltz King" of Vienna, increased the number of metronome beats per measure and transmuted the even beat of three counts into one in which the first beat was overemphasized and the second beat was understressed. The younger Strauss, and the many musical composers who followed his rhythmic pattern, brought waltz music to a peak of musical and technical perfection. The Viennese Waltz, as it came to be known to the world, demanded even greater skill and endurance than had the earlier, slower form. Because of the increased tempo, the entire dance was performed up on the toes. Dancers held their middle-bodies in rigidly controlled postures. The posture, no doubt, was aided by the lavish, and tight fitting, military uniforms affected by the gentlemen of that era. The ladies' ball gowns were equally as snug with tightly laced and corseted bodices.

The Viennese Waltz enjoyed a long reign as queen of the ballroom. It was not until the threat of World War I that the Viennese version of the waltz began to fade into a world of comic opera memories, beautiful and unreal. As World War I became a reality, all nations not allied with Germany declared that anything stemming from or reflecting Germanic influence and culture was anathema.

Among dancers, however, the waltz was too popular a favorite to be forgotten entirely. New melodies replaced the old ones and the tempo was again decreased. The accent returned to the even three-beat that had been used in the older Ländler rhythms. The slower rhythm again permitted the dancers occasionally to place the flat foot upon the floor to sustain balance. An attempt was made to change the name of the dance to *The Boston,* but it was a thin disguise and was soon dropped. Dancing teams, such as the famous Irene and Vernon Castle, introduced new figures to the slower tempo which would not have been possible to perform in the rapid rhythm of the Viennese mode. Some of these variations have been retained in the American Waltz, as the dance has come to be termed, but it remains essentially one characterized by turning and gliding figures. The mood of the American Waltz has also altered into one expressing a more romantic and dreamy quality than was evident in the Viennese form. While not as fast as its Austrian ancestor, the American Waltz is still a complex dance requiring knowledge, practice, and skill to perform.

Because of the complexities of the Waltz, it should be presented to the students early in the teaching schedule. Well-marked music of a moderate tempo is preferable for the initial teaching sessions. A tempo that is too slow requires sustained movements. For inexperienced dancers this is more difficult than attempting to keep up with a fast rhythm. The instructor should make certain that the music used is played by a *dance* orchestra and not by a symphonic orchestra.

STYLING   The American Waltz requires good posture for both partners. Each must support his own weight as he dances in the face-to-face position which originated with the Waltz. With only rare exceptions the closed position is maintained throughout the dance. In the turning figures, especially, the man must lead his partner strongly so that she is directly in front of him at all times.

A subtle fall and rise in the bodies of the dancers as they follow the accents of the music is an important characteristic of the Waltz. This is accomplished by stepping flat upon the sole of the foot during the accented beat of the music and slightly relaxing the knee. For the following two beats of the measure the dancers lift themselves, initiating the lift from within the middle body, to rise lightly upon their toes. As the waltzers become more experienced and relaxed, a subtle side-to-side swaying motion should develop in the upper body and shoulders. The swaying motion grows from extending, or reaching, the accented step a little farther than the following two steps. All body movements must remain smooth and finely controlled so that no exaggerated motion results.

The feet of both dancers remain close to the floor to create the desired illusion of gliding. All progressive figures in the American Waltz flow forward in a counter-clockwise line around the dancing area.

RHYTHM ANALYSIS   Waltz music is written in 3/4 time, indicating three beats to each measure; therefore, three steps to every measure in the dance. Each of the three counts is of *equal duration*. The first note in each measure is accented to distinguish it from the following two counts. Without the accented beat the dancer would soon become confused as to which was the initial count and the dance would become completely disorganized.

A graphic diagram of two measures of Waltz looks like this:

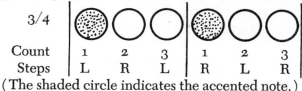

3/4						
Count	1	2	3	1	2	3
Steps	L	R	L	R	L	R

(The shaded circle indicates the accented note.)

While the tempo of the Waltz may be slow, medium, or fast, the rhythm is consistent throughout each selection. The Waltz is the only dance which cannot be counted in a combination of slow and quick counts.

TEACHING PROGRESSIONS   Listen to several selections of Waltzes in slow, medium, and fast tempos. Have the students mark the accented beat in some manner such as snapping their fingers, clapping hands, or counting aloud.

After they are able to distinguish the accent, move the students into the dancing area to begin working, without partners, on the footwork of the Waltz. The foot pattern consists of a series of three changes of weight placed basically in a triangular form. When two of the triangles are placed together, one beginning forward and the other backward, or in the reverse order, a a square pattern of movement results. With the development of the square into a turning figure it loses its triangular form but the essential three changes of weight are retained.

The Waltz Square, also termed a Waltz Box, is an easy beginning figure. If the students have previously learned the Box formation in the Argentine Tango (beginning of Figure II) they will already be familiar with the foot pattern. The rhythm and styling differs, however, when the Square or Box figure is used in the Waltz.

Waltz Square (Forward Half)

	Count
Step fwd. on LF	1
Bring RF fwd. near LF then step out to right side on RF	2
(A small arc, or semi-circular movement of the leg is made as the leg swings fwd. and out to the side on this count.)	
Close LF beside RF, transferring weight to LF	3

Note that each time a foot is moved, full weight is placed upon it.

Walk through the backward half of the Waltz Square:

Waltz Square (Backward Half)

	Count
Step bkwd. on RF	1
Bring LF bkwd. near RF then step out to left side on LF	2
(This movement is the reverse of the arc, or semi-circular leg swing made in the Forward Half on the corresponding count.)	
Close RF to LF, transferring weight to RF	3

Without regard to styling, walk through both figures until they are comprehended. The most frequent error occurs on the 3rd count when students fail to transfer their weight to the foot taking that count.

Reverse the exercise to begin the Waltz Square by leading backward with the right foot on the initial count.

Bring to the students' attention the fact that one triangular pattern, the forward half, begins with the *toe* of the left foot leading *forward*. The other pattern, or backward half, begins with the *heel* of the right foot leading *backward*. This knowledge will be important when the men and women are ready to dance together in closed position, and also for the later development of the turning figures.

After the pattern of the Waltz Square has become familiar the fall and rise of the body may be added. During the practice of the exercise make certain that the students retain a good, but not stiff, posture. The middle body should remain controlled but not overly constricted. Both men and women should practice without partners.

Body Fall and Rise

	Count
Step fwd. on flat foot of LF, letting left knee bend very slightly. Full body weight is over LF	1
Step to right side with RF, observing the arc pattern of movement. As the weight is transferred over the RF, the body is lifted slightly so that only the forward part of the foot is resting on the floor. The lift is made from the middle, or diaphragm area of the body.	2
Retain the lift in the body, close LF beside RF, transferring weight to forward part of LF	3

Reverse the figure by stepping back on the right foot on the accented beat. The sole of the right shoe should be flat upon the floor and the right knee bent slightly. Continue counts two and three as in the Backward half of the Waltz Square, lifting the body and sustaining the lift for those two counts.

Verbally cue the sequence as, "Flat, lift, lift."

To gain coordination of footwork and the body movement, let

the students practice individually to a recording of moderate tempo.

After sufficient individual practice the students may take partners and practice the Waltz Square together, using closed ballroom position. The man must lead the woman into the exact counterpart of his footwork; as he steps forward he leads her into stepping backward.

The Waltz Square is the key figure to all that will follow in the dance and should be thoroughly understood by the dancers before one introduces new figures. This includes the proper fall and rise of the body, correct timing with the rhythm, and accurate use of leading or following techniques.

Reverse the entire exercise by having the men begin the Waltz Square stepping backward with their right foot. The figure may begin in either manner and both methods should be given sufficient practice to assure their adroit usage.

"*Step*, side, close," is a useful verbal cue to direct the footwork of both dancers in closed position.

To travel in the Waltz, the same triangular patterns are used that formed the half-square. The important difference is that the triangles do not alternately move forward and backward, but are directed in one course around the dancing area. The traveling figure is frequently termed the Pursuit Waltz.

For practice, have both men and women, without partners, turn to face the line of direction. Both may use the same footwork.

Pursuit Waltz

	Count	Weight
Step fwd. on LF	1	flat
Step out to right side (making arc) on RF	2	lift
Close LF to RF (transferring weight)	3	lift
Step fwd. on RF	1	flat
Step out to left side (making arc) on LF	2	lift
Close RF to LF (transferring weight)	3	lift

To lend a little additional styling while practicing the traveling figure, have the students take a comfortably long step forward on each count of 1. The dancers should experience the feeling of initiating the movement from the hip rather than from the knee or ankle. Verbally, this may be called, "Reach, side, close."

When the forward Pursuit Waltz has become familiar, have the students turn their backs to the line of direction and reverse the entire figure. They will still be moving in the traditional counterclockwise path of movement around the room but will be traveling backwards. The long, reaching step on the count of 1 should also be used as they travel backwards.

With partners, practice the Pursuit Waltz until it is comfortable. Begin by having the men face the line of direction. As the men move forward they lead the women into the counterpart of their footwork so that the women travel backwards.

After sufficient practice, reverse the positions so that the man has his back to the line of direction. The man will travel backward and the lady forward. While this position is a difficult one for the man to lead with authority and control until he has gained experience, it should be practiced for a few measures. It will serve to emphasize that it is permissible for the man to travel backwards in the Waltz if he so desires.

For an easy practice sequence, alternate four measures of the Waltz Square with four measures of the Pursuit Waltz. Practice the sequence until the students are able to move from one figure into another without difficulty.

The instructor must be sure that all points regarding rhythm, fall and rise, and leading or following techniques are being obeyed as well as the footwork patterns.

Allow the students to make their own sequence by using *any* number of measures of the Waltz Square combined with *any* number of measures of the Pursuit Waltz. Because the responsibility of creating the sequence falls to the men, they must concentrate upon making *clear* and *positive* leads if they expect their partners to respond properly. In a two-figure sequence the men will soon experience the correct use of their hands and bodies to lead effectively.

Turning figures in the Waltz may revolve in either direction. In a *left* turn the dancers are moving in a *counterclockwise* direction, and a *right* turn revolves them in a *clockwise* direction. In operating an automobile the driver learns that he must turn the wheels to the left to make a left turn, or to the right to make a right turn. The same principle applies to making a turn in dancing. For the beginning dancer, the easiest manner of turning to the left is to lead with the toes of his left foot pointing outward to the left as he makes the first step. The dancer then continues to turn toward that direction. To make a right, or clockwise, turn, the dancer leads out with the toe of the right foot turned toward the right. When the turn is performed in place it is known as a Box Turn. It is essentially the same as the Waltz Square, but with the development of the turning movement.

Working individually, have both men and women walk through the following exercise:

Box Turn, Left (Counterclockwise)

	Count
Step fwd. on LF, toe turned *out* to left, making ¼ turn left (CCW)	1
Step to side, making arc as in Waltz Square, on RF	2
Close LF to RF, changing weight to LF	3
Step bkwd. on RF, toe turned *in* to left, (heel out), making ¼ turn left (CCW)	1
Step to side, making arc as in Waltz Square, on LF	2
Close RF to LF, changing weight to RF	3

If the dancer has been making a quarter-turn on each three counts, it will take four measures, or 12 beats, to make a complete revolution. For beginning students the degree of the turn should not be overly stressed as long as the direction of the turn is correct. The dancers observe that the count of *one* is important in establishing the direction for the turn. The rule applies whether the first step is taken forward with the toe turned *out,* or is initiated by leading backward with the toe turned *in.*

Repeat the exercise and add the correct *flat, lift, lift,* body motion. The first count may also be accented by reaching forward or backward with a long step.

The directional cue of, "Turn, side, close," may be used with the exercise.

After sufficient individual practice with music, have the dancers rejoin their partners in closed position. In turning figures in the Waltz, the man must keep his partner directly in front of himself as they revolve together. The common error is for the man to attempt to step around his partner.

In closed position the woman performs the exact counterpart of the man's steps. As the man steps forward on his left foot with toe turned out, he must lead his partner into stepping back on her right foot with her toe turned in (heel out). The Box Turn revolves in a small area in place, in either direction. The students should not attempt to make the figure travel.

After sufficient practice in turning to the left (counterclockwise) in the Box Turn, make a practice sequence of four measures of Pursuit Waltz steps alternating with four measures of Box Turns, revolving left. Follow this exercise by letting the men lead their own sequence of the same two figures.

Without partners, walk through the Box Turn to the *right*, revolving clockwise. Begin by having both men and women step forward on their right foot with the toe of that foot turned out to the right. The directions are the reverse of those given for the Box Turn to the left. The turn to the right (clockwise) is usually more difficult for dancers to accomplish. For this reason it may be necessary to spend more time upon it than was needed for the left turn.

There are two methods of changing the direction of turning figures in the Waltz. Experienced dancers are able to accomplish the change by using an odd number of measures, three, five, seven, turning to the left. As the man's right foot becomes free he quickly shifts the direction of the turn to the right by quickly leading forward with his right foot.

With beginning dancers it is easier to use one of two figures which serves as connecting links. One figure is known as the Waltz Balance, and the other the Waltz Hesitation. Both figures retain the rhythm of the Waltz, but the footwork varies from the basic triangular pattern. The student may use whichever is most comfortable, but should be familiar with both.

Waltz Balance

(Directions for man, woman does counterpart when in
closed position.)

	Count	Weight
Step fwd. on LF	1	flat
Close RF to LF, raising on ball of RF	2	lift
Transfer weight to LF, maintaining lift in body	3	lift
Step bkwd. on RF	1	flat
Close LF to RF, raising on ball of LF	2	lift
Transfer weight to RF, maintaining lift in body	3	lift

Waltz Hesitation

(Directions for man, woman does counterpart when in
closed position.)

	Count	Weight
Step fwd. on LF	1	flat
Close toe of RF beside LF, making slight body lift, but *without* transfer of weight	2	lift
Hold same position	3	hold
Step bkwd. on RF	1	flat
Close toe of LF beside RF, making slight body lift, but *without* transfer of weight	2	lift
Hold same position	3	hold

The steps in either the Waltz Balance or the Waltz Hesitation should be small. Each figure may be performed beginning forward, backward, or from side to side.

As a practice sequence make a combination of *four* measures of Box Turns, turning left; *three* measures of either Walz Balance or Waltz Hesitation; and *four* measures of the Box Turn, turning right. Walk through the combination to count, making certain that the students understand the purpose of the connecting Waltz Balance or Waltz Hesitation is to free one foot to effect a change of direction in the Box Turn. Practice with music.

Eventually repeat a similar exercise using only *one* measure of the connecting Waltz Balance or Waltz Hesitation.

The Extended Turn is similar to the Box Turn except a full half-turn is made in place of the quarter degree, or less, turn. This movement causes the dancers to progress in a straight line of direction as they revolve. For the first practice sessions on the Extended Turns move all the dancers to one side of the hall and ask them to perform the initial exercises moving in a straight line *across* the hall. This procedure assists the students to keep a clearer sense of direction than is possible in trying to move in a circle.

For the practice session, both men and women may use the same footwork. They begin by facing the wall of the opposite side of the hall, which becomes their temporary line of direction.

Extended Turn, Left (Counterclockwise)

	Count
Step fwd. on LF in LOD, making ¼ turn to left (toe turned *out*)	1
Step sdwd. on RF in LOD, continuing ¼ turn to left (dancers' backs should now be to LOD, having made a full ½ turn.)	2
Close LF to RF, transferring weight to LF	3
Step bkwd. on RF in LOD, making ¼ turn to left (toe turned *in*)	1
Step sdwd. on LF in LOD, continuing ¼ turn to left (dancers should now be facing original LOD.)	2
Close RF to LF, transferring weight to RF	3

A strong, definite leading step in the desired line of direction, whether leading forward or backward, keeps the figure moving in a straight line.

After having walked through the figure and then individually practiced the Extended Turn to music, students may practice with partners. The woman performs the exact counterpart of the man's steps. Practice the turn moving across the hall.

In any turning figure in dancing caution the students to keep their eyes on a normal eye-level. By looking at the floor or at their feet they heighten the sensation of dizziness which is normal in a series of turns. Eventually, as they become more experienced and expert, the dancers should become familiar with the principle of "spotting" in turning, or pivoting, sequences. This is achieved by the dancers keeping their eyes trained upon a "spot," either real or imaginary, in the line of direction in which they are moving. In doing this the head faces one direction as long as possible before it is quickly turned to again look at the "spot." Because the head revolves at a slower rate of speed than the body, dizziness is avoided.

The Right Extended Turn (clockwise) is the reverse of the turn to the left. Practice this individually, with both men and women beginning by stepping forward in the line of direction on the right foot, turning right (clockwise), and traveling in a straight line across the floor as they individually revolve.

After practicing the right turn, both individually and with partners, use a series of turning figures in the traditional counterclockwise line of direction around the hall. First, practice a series of Extended Turns to the left, having the men begin with their left foot. Next, practice the Extended Turn to the right, having the men begin by leading forward on their right foot.

In making a turning figure in the Waltz, either the Box Turn or the Extended Turn, it is necessary for the man to hold his partner securely with his right arm, making the hold correspondingly tighter and more secure when the tempo of the music is increased. As the tempo of the music is *increased,* the size of the steps must become *correspondingly smaller* to keep up with the rhythm. In a turning figure, this also increases the speed with which the dancers revolve. It will enhance the appearance of the dancing couple to have each partner pull his shoulders backward to a slight degree as they are turning.

As a practice combination, use *four* measures of Extended Turn to the *left* (counterclockwise); *three* Waltz Balance *or* Waltz Hesitation figures *in place; four* measures of the Extended Turn to the *right* (clockwise). Make certain that the Extended Turns progress and do not become Box Turns in place.

Repeat a similar exercise using *one* connecting figure between the Extended Turns.

Permit the students to create their own sequence of Extended Turns, in both directions, connected by the Balance or Hesitation figures.

Next, ask the students to create a free sequence combining *all* the figures they have practiced in the Waltz. The sequence should include the *Waltz Square;* the *Pursuit Waltz; Box Turns,* both to the right and left; *Extended Turns*, to the right and left; and the connecting *Balance* and Hesitation figures. As the students practice, the instructor should observe that they are following the correct rhythm and applying the proper styling.

All turning figures may be initiated by the man stepping *backward* instead of forward as has been done in the practice exercises. If the man wishes to turn left (counterclockwise), he leads back on his *right* foot, with the toe of that foot turned strongly *inward* to the left. He may begin a right turn (clockwise) by leading backward on his *left* foot, the toe of that foot pointing *inward* to the right. At the same time, he leads his partner into making the counter movement.

Practice the technique of initiating turns with the man leading backward until they are executed easily.

A simple variation which retains the form of the Pursuit Step, but creates a different appearance, is the Diagonal Crossover figure. In some schools and studios the figure is also called the Weaving or Waving variation. The figure should be used only with music of a slow or moderate tempo. In a fast Waltz the figure loses the grace and dignity which it requires. The figure also presents its best form when it is used as a traveling figure and not one danced in place.

Diagonal Crossover

Count

Partners facing in closed position:

Man steps diagonally fwd. on LF, his left leg crossing between self and partner, bringing their left hips adjacent } 1
Woman steps diagonally bkwd. on RF

Man steps swd. to right on RF } 2
Woman steps swd. to left on LF

Man closes LF to RF, transferring weight to LF } 3
Woman closes RF to LF, transferring weight to RF

On counts 2 and 3, the dancers turn slightly toward partners, ending face-to-face on final count.

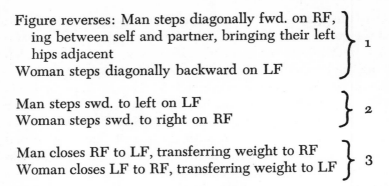

Figure reverses: Man steps diagonally fwd. on RF, ⎫
   ing between self and partner, bringing their left ⎬ 1
   hips adjacent
Woman steps diagonally backward on LF ⎭

Man steps swd. to left on LF ⎫
Woman steps swd. to right on RF ⎬ 2

Man closes RF to LF, transferring weight to RF ⎫
Woman closes LF to RF, transferring weight to LF ⎬ 3

    Both turning slightly on cts. 2 and 3 to face partners again.

    In the Diagonal Crossover figure, the man must lead his partner strongly so that she steps diagonally backward as he steps diagonally forward. If desired, the entire figure may be reversed with the man leading backward. The *flat, lift, lift,* body movement must be maintained in the figure. The first count, the crossing step, must not be allowed to develop into a dip.

    In all figures in the Waltz, the upper body should be carried proudly erect and with dignity. The entire dance should create an impression of effortless gliding and turning to the even cadence of the Waltz rhythm.

CHAPTER SEVEN

HEEL AND TOE POLKA

BACKGROUND   "First your heel and then your toe, that's the way the polka goes!" Those were the lilting lyrics to a song inspired by the Polka upon the introduction of that dance to the United States in 1844.

As with many other dances that have become popular favorites, the origin of the Polka is so obscured by legends and folk lore that exacting facts are difficult to extricate. One of the most prevalent theories states that in 1830 a musician and teacher of dancing in Bohemia (now Czechoslovakia), observed a young servant girl singing and dancing to an improvised melody. The musician, Josef Neruda, was so impressed by the joyous, light-hearted quality of the song and dance that he immediately made a notation of both. The dance was eventually taught in Prague, where it received the name "Polka." Authorities disagree as to the meaning of the name; some stating that it derived from the Czech word *pulka,* meaning *half,* while an equal force of vehement researchers defend their view that the name signifies *Polish Girl.*

Whatever the meaning of the name or the true beginning of the dance, it gained almost instantaneous acclaim wherever it made its appearance in Europe. The Polka was first introduced into Paris as part of a ballet sequence in an opera performance. The young dancers of the corps de ballet were so enthralled by the Polka that they insisted upon dancing it at the public balls. It caught the immediate attention of the Parisian dancing masters as well as the dancing public who were eager to welcome any innovation. Polka Academies mushroomed in Paris and the surrounding provinces, each dancing master professing to be the only one offering instructions in the "original Polka." The fact that most of them created their own interpretations of the dance undoubtedly accounts for some of the many forms which still exist.

In some schools it was taught as a formal dance, following the form of the quadrille and consisting of a series of figures prompted by a master of ceremonies. In others, the Polka became a solo dance to be performed with improvised inventiveness and abandon.

From Paris, the Polka hopped and skipped the length and breadth of Europe. It permeated all levels of society, even becoming entrenched in the older folk dance forms of many nations. The professional theatre also adopted the Polka and inserted alluring variations into every production.

The Polka did not linger long in making the stride across the Atlantic to the New World, with various interpretations being offered in Mexico City, New Orleans, New York, and Boston. As the tide of American civilization expanded westward across new states and territories, the Polka was favored by intrepid pioneers as a welcome diversion around evening campfires or in the sheltering protection of trading posts which had become established along remote trailways. In the Mother Lode country of California, and in Colorado's Pike's Peak region, hordes of seekers of precious ore danced the lively Polka in hastily constructed shacks lining dusty streets of new communities bearing colorful names such as Hangtown, Poker Flat, Angel's Camp, Leadville, and Cripple Creek.

The popularity of the Polka survived in the United States until the Civil War period when it faded simultaneously from the salons of fashionable society and the saloons of the less affluent. Far from being dead, however, the dance continues to revive with renewed vigor whenever a new Polka tune stirs the memories of older generations of dancers or titilates the feet of younger ones into action.

The many variations of the Polka have always been favorites of youthful dancers and it is used frequently in ski lodges, summer resorts, or other centers of activity esteemd as gathering places.

STYLING   Unless the dancer is attempting to emulate one of the many ethnic forms of the Polka, it may be as ebullient or as subdued as he wishes to make it. Some dancers enjoy exaggerating the hop, others elide it almost completely.

Because the tempo of the Polka is lively, the length of each step needs to be comparatively short to keep in pace with the music. To achieve the required body lightness, dancers lift themselves upward from the center of their bodies allowing the weight to rest on the forward part of the feet as they take each step. The "hop" need not be a literal jump, but only an additional inner lift which creates an upward emphasis.

Various positions may be taken in holding partners for the Polka. These include the traditional ballroom position, shoulder-waist position, or several varieties of open positions in which the dancers face a common direction. The open position has the added advantage of permitting three people to Polka together, in any combination of sexes. In the Polka threesome, the leader is the dancer in the center who directs the other two by placing his (or her) arms behind their backs; they place their inside hands upon the nearest shoulder of the leader. By use of the triple formation, every student should be able to participate in the Polka.

RHYTHM ANALYSIS   Polka music is customarily written in 2/4 time, meaning that there are two musical beats to the measure. The dance pattern, however, requires four parts. To accomplish this, the two slow beats are divided to make a total of four quick beats per measure, as illustrated in the following two-measure diagram:

2/4				
Count	1-&	2-&	1-&	2-&
Rhythm	Q Q	Q Q	Q Q	Q Q
Steps	L R	L hop	R L	R hop

TEACHING PROGRESSIONS   Develop the footwork of the Polka from simple walking steps, temporarily ignoring the correct styling and timing.

With all students facing the line of direction and both men and women using the same footwork, take three normal walking steps forward and pause in place on the fourth count. The objective is to establish the proper change of weight which may be counted: "left, right, left, hold; right, left, right, hold." Continue for a short time, calling the footwork at a slow, even cadence.

Next, develop the same change of weight pattern into one frequently termed the "two-step." Beginning with the left foot, take a normal step forward on the count of 1; on the count of 2, bring the right foot forward approximately even with the left foot and transfer the weight onto the right foot; on the count of 3, take a normal step forward on the left foot; hold in place on the count of 4, without any change of weight. Reverse the procedure to begin the next four counts by stepping forward with the right foot. The sequence may be verbally cued as: "long, short, long, hold," or "step, close, step, hold." Although the second step is shorter than the other two, the same change of weight should be used as in the three walking steps. A common fault among students is to fail to place their weight upon the second, or short step.

After the first part of the figure has been mastered, change the "hold" into a "hop" on the count of 4. The "hop" results from an inner lifting of the body and does not have to be large. Change the verbal cue to: "long, short, long, hop," or "step, close, step, hop." Without partners, practice the completed sequence, gradually increasing the tempo of the verbal cues to approximate that of a moderate Polka. After the footwork has been established, and as the tempo increases, the rhythmic cue of "one, and, two, and" is usually sufficient to keep the dancers moving with precision.

Listen to parts of several recordings of Polka music to permit the students to become familiar with the instrumental music and to associate the footwork with it. Ask the students to practice without partners to a short selection of Polka music. The instructor should observe that the footwork is light and that the dancers' bodies are carried in a buoyant manner.

Request dancers to take partners in any open position such as the Varsovienne, or the Skaters hold (see illustrations). Three dancers may dance together, the center person being the leader of the other two. When any of the open positions are used in Polka, *all* dancers will begin with the *left* foot. Practice the basic footwork with partners for a few measures of recorded music.

HEEL AND TOE

Because the Polka moves forward at a lively pace, it is desirable to break the constant flow by adding a figure which permits the dancers to orient themselves. One of the most popular figures is the Heel and Toe variation. It uses the same rhythm and styling as in the basic Polka figure. Eight measures of the basic Polka are alternated with eight measures of the Heel and Toe figure. Instructors should be certain to use recordings that are played with the eight-measure phrase, and avoid those which have inserts of two or four measure interludes.

In open position, both men and women use the same footwork for the Heel and Toe figure.

Steps	*Count*	*Verbal Cue*
Extend LF diag. fwd. and touch *heel* to floor, toe pointing upward	1	Heel
Hop in place on RF	&	—
Bring LF back to touch *toe* to floor beside RF	2	Toe
Hop in place on RF	&	—
Step fwd. on LF	1	Step
Close RF to LF, transferring weight	&	Close
Step fwd. on LF	2	Step
Hop in place on LF	&	—

Reverse the entire sequence to begin with right foot extended forward, touching *heel* to floor.

The entire figure must be performed a total of four times, alternately beginning left; right; left; right; to correspond to the eight-measure phrasing of the music.

For the first few sessions in which the Heel and Toe figure is alternated with the basic Polka, a more controlled flow of traffic may be gained by directing all students to use the same figure at the same time. After they have gained experience and skill, each couple may then begin with its own choice of figures.

After the dancers have gained mastery of the Heel and Toe Polka in open position, they will enjoy the same sequence in the slightly more difficult closed position. The framework of the dance is the same in both positions, but in closed position the Polka figure is performed with each couple revolving clockwise while traveling in a general counterclockwise path around the dancing area.

To aid in establishing a clear sense of direction, move all of the students to one end of the hall and practice the revolving Polka step in straight lines down the length of the hall. Dancers practice without partners, and both men and women use the same footwork for the initial exercises.

With all dancers standing with their *left* side toward the empty end of the hall, slowly walk through the turning Polka figure. Each dancer should turn constantly to his own right (clockwise). It requires one measure to make *half* a revolution.

Steps	*Count*
Meas. 1 Begin CW turn by stepping diag. *fwd.* on LF with toe turned *inward*	1
Close RF to LF, transferring wt. to RF while continuing to turn CW	&
Step diag. bkwd. on LF, continuing to turn CW	2
Hop in place on LF, making small pivot in place to complete ½ of CW revolution (Dancer's *right* side should now be toward empty end of hall.)	&
Meas. 2 Continue turning CW by stepping diag. *bkwd.* on RF with toe turned *inward*	1
Close LF to RF, transferring wt. to LF, continuing to turn CW	&
Step diag. fwd. on RF, continuing CW turn	2
Hop in place on RF, making small pivot in place to complete turn	&

(At the end of the 2nd measure, the dancer should have

completed one CW revolution and traveled a short distance in the LOD.)

Each count of 1 must be made generally toward the line of direction.

With dancers continuing to work individually, repeat the turning Polka to count; then to music until the technique of the continuous turning becomes clear.

When the students are ready to dance with partners, have them assume the shoulder-waist position. This position assists them in maintaining the necessary relationship in which each dancer's shoulders and hips must remain parallel to those of his partner as they turn together. Hold arms firmly to give the necessary support.

In closed position, the man begins with his *left* foot, stepping diagonally forward toward his partner, as in the directions for *measure 1* of the written description. The lady begins with her *right* foot, stepping diagonally backward, as in the directions for *measure 2*. Because the clockwise turn is initiated by turning the toes inward on the count of 1, that step must be executed with confidence and decision. After the revolution has been properly started, it is not difficult to keep the figure turning.

Permit the dancing couples to practice the clockwise turning figure traveling the length of the hall; then practice it moving in the standard counterclockwise path of movement around the hall.

In the closed position, the Heel and Toe variation also changes from that used in the open position. The footwork remains essentially the same, but all movements are *sideward*. The man begins with his *left* foot, extending it sideward to touch the *heel* to the floor; the lady does the counterpart, beginning with her *right* foot extended to her right side. Both bring their extended foot back to touch the toe beside the standing foot. Both make a Polka step moving sideward to the man's left. The entire figure then reveress to begin toward his right side; then repeats to his left; then reverses to his right side.

To assist in alleviating the dizziness which results from the Polka, or any rapidly turning dance, dancers must avoid looking downward toward the floor. They will find the faces of their partners much more interesting!

CHAPTER EIGHT

SWING
(Lindy, Shag, Jitterbug)

BACKGROUND   Charles Lindbergh, a young aviator, became famous overnight when he flew a small plane from New York City to Paris, France, in 1927. His was the first solo flight across the Atlantic, and the young "Lindy" became the unwitting hero of the entire world. Among the countless accolades conferred upon the modest hero was the creation of a new dance bearing the title *Lindy Hop*. It was literally a "hop," performed to fast Fox Trot music and accented the syncopated, or "off" beat in the music. The Lindy Hop grew into a popular feature in the dance palaces and ballrooms of the New York City area, but failed to gain wide acceptance in other areas of the United States. It did, however, have a strong influence upon dances which developed later.

One of these was the *Shag*. The Shag was danced in a cheek-to-cheek position with clasped hands held in an exaggerated fashion high above the heads. The dancers' feet swung like pendulums as they hopped forward or backward or from side to side in a series of quick-quick-slow rhythms. The dance was extremely popular with college students.

Another dance influenced by the Lindy Hop was the *Jitterbug*. Jitterbug originated in New York's Harlem district as an exhibition dance which involved exuberant acrobatics and perfectly timed teamwork on the part of the dancers. The Jitterbug also became a featured novelty in the endurance contests which offered a small promise of monetary gain to unemployed dancers during the financial debacle of the mid-1930's. The contests, termed Dance Marathons, not only required each participating

couple to dance for endless hours without stopping, but also, during exhibition "sprints," to entertain the paying audience with a display of the Jitterbug.

Because Jitterbug expressed a vivacious, youthful quality, it had a strong appeal to the teen-age dancers who adapted it to ballroom use. Many areas, and even local neighborhoods, developed forms which were strictly original and unique from the figures used in other areas. Because the dance was completely ignored by dance teacher organizations, it never developed a standard form of performance.

During the 1930's, although it was a decade of financial failures and unemployment, ballroom dancing attained a greater degree of popularity and finesse than had ever been experienced in the United States. It was the era of the Big Dance Bands, and every community possessed its public dance hall. In their effort to establish an individual identity, many of the orchestras experimented in creating new and distinguishing sounds and rhythms. Some orchestra leaders found that the predominately favorite Fox Trot rhythm could be made into a more "swinging" rhythm by shifting the accents from counts 1 and 3, to counts 2 and 4. Dancers of the Lindy Hop, Shag, and Jitterbug, were quick to discover that the new rhythm gave their dances an added lilt that had not been possible with the smoother Fox Trot rhythm. Before long, all dances of the same general pattern came to be identified as *Swing Dances*. In slang parlance, the music was termed "jive," and the devotees of dances in the new rhythms were classed as "hepcats."

The newer "Swing" dance developed a more standard form of execution based upon figures from the older Jitterburg and Lindy dances. The term "Lindy" is still retained to identify the basic footwork patterns.

During World War II, G. I. Joes carried the new dances to the many battle fronts of that conflict. The young people of those countries were intrigued by both the music and the dances and quickly adopted them as their own even when they represented a total departure from the native music and dance.

Swing has become an established dance in the American repertory of popular dancing and retains a strong appeal to dancers of all ages. It is a versatile dance that can be fitted to the music of either the older Fox Trot, Swing rhythm, or the more current Rock 'n Roll sound. Stylewise, it may vary from flamboyant to conservative.

STYLING Swing has a styling distinctly its own and is equally as vital to the dance as the footwork. Although the acrobatic stunts which made the early Jitterbug form of the dance so sensational have long been discarded, the same keen cooperation of timing and coordinated response from both partners is still a necessary part of Swing. Alone, the footwork can be vapidly dull, but when the footwork and proper arm and body movements are combined to achieve the desired interaction between two partners, the dance literally springs with vitality. Whether the dance is performed in a subdued manner or in a more athletic fashion, the same sense of controlled interplay needs to be achieved by both partners.

The entire upper torso of both dancers must swing, either

forward and backward, or from side to side, with a sense of counter resistance; the arms retain an elastic quality of flexibility as the man pulls his partner toward him and then pushes her back to end the figure with a fast, surprising reversal of the same movements.

Contemporary Swing differs from other popular dances in that the lady *does not* perform the exact counterpart of the man's footwork. Although she uses the opposite foot, she steps *forward* at the same time the man moves *forward*, and *backward* as he steps *backward*. An integral part of the dance is the spring-like use of the arms which keeps the partners moving together and apart similar to rubber bands being stretched and relaxed. If the arms are allowed to relax completely, or are not used correctly, the dance dies like the rubber band which has lost its snap.

Dancers may use challenge position with one or both hands joined across, or may use open ballroom position. In challenge position, the footwork moves generally forward and backward; in open position, because of the closeness of the dancers, the footwork moves from side to side. All steps are made in a flat, earthy manner and are short in length, permitting partners to remain together as they dance in a "spot."

MUSICAL ANALYSIS   Although there are many versions of Swing, the dance pattern that has become generally accepted throughout the United States requires *six* beats of music. The music may be written in either 4/4 or 2/4 time, but should have a definite "two-beat" rhythm. In 4/4 time, the dance sequence takes one and one-half measures of music; in 2/4 time, it requires three measures.

A three-measure chart of the Single Lindy, the foundation combination of the dance, is diagrammed here:

2/4						
Count	1	2	3	4	5	6
Rhythm	S		S		Q	Q
Man's Steps	L	hold	R	hold	L	R
Lady's Steps	R	hold	L	hold	R	L

The *man* always begins the sequence with his *left* foot; the lady always starts with her *right*. The music may be counted as: 1-2 1-2, 1-2, 1-2, indefinitely throughout the selection. Because of the various methods of shifting the accents to produce swing rhythm, the count of 1 may not always be the accented count, but in most music that initial beat is easy to distinguish. Individual couples may begin their six-count combination on *any* count of *1*

TEACHING PROGRESSIONS   Have the group listen to parts of several recordings of Swing music in slow, moderate, and fast tempos. Point out the musical phrasing which must always be in units of two beats. Although some Fox Trot music is suitable for Swing, it is better to use music with a more pronounced rhythm for beginning dancers. When the students indicate their understanding of the rhythm by counting or clapping, move them to the dancing area to begin working on the steps of the foundation sequence.

With the men in one line, and the ladies in an opposite line facing the men, briefly teach the basic footwork to each individual line. Initially, concentrate upon footwork rather than body styling.

The *men* use the following footwork:

Steps	Count	Rhythm
Short step fwd. on flat of LF	1	S
Hold LF in place	2	
Short step bkwd. on flat of RF	3	S
Hold RF in place	4	
Short step bkwd. on LF (toe turned out and trunk of body slightly twisted to left)	5	Q
Step in place on RF (turning body to face fwd.)	6	Q

, Repeat the footwork several times to make certain the students understand the six-count dance phrase.

Next, teach the footwork to the ladies in their line:

Steps	Count	Rhythm
Short step fwd. on flat of RF	1	S
Hold RF in place	2	
Short step bkwd. on flat of LF	3	S
Hold LF in place	4	

Short step bkwd. on RF (toe turned out and trunk
   of body slightly twisted to right)   5   Q
Step in place on LF (turning body to face fwd.)   6   Q

Repeat the footwork several times for the benefit of the ladies. It is important for them to understand that they step *forward* at the same time the men move forward. Because this movement is contrary to the rules of most standard dances, the exception must be clearly delineated.

When each line knows its individual steps, both lines may practice simultaneously to the verbal cue of "forward-hold, back-hold, quick, quick", or a similar directional call corresponding to the *slow, slow, quick, quick,* rhythm. Retain the lines and practice the basic footwork to recorded music; all dancers beginning at the same time on cue from the instructor.

When both men and women have learned to associate the footwork with the rhythm, begin working on the characteristic body styling and unite it with the basic footwork.

On the slow counts, the action of the upper body is slightly delayed and does not move over the foot until *after* the weight has been placed on the foot.

With men and women in their individual lines, simultaneously work on the following exercise at a slow tempo; men beginning with left foot, ladies with right foot:

a. Short step fwd. with knee bent and pelvis slightly tucked under as if beginning to sit down;

b. Push the upper body forward from the middle of the body until the body is over the standing foot with the knee and pelvis straightened.

Reverse the procedure:

a. Short step bkwd. with knee relaxed and pelvis tucked under;

b. Pull the upper body backward from the middle of the body until it is over the standing foot with the knee and pelvis straightened.

The desired effect should resemble the resistance experienced in taking a step forward or backward in a shoulder-deep pool of water.

Practice the slow forward and backward movement to a verbal count, gradually increasing the tempo until it approximates that of slow or moderate Swing rhythm. As the tempo increases, the footwork becomes lighter with a slight bouncy effect resulting from the knee action. Repeat the practice of the forward and backward movement to a few measures of recorded music. The instructor must stress the proper use of the knees and the hips. Swing movement cannot be gained with wooden-soldier bodies and legs.

The *quick* counts of 5 and 6 are less complex, but require a brief analysis. Beginning to the man's left side with his left foot, and to the lady's right side with her right foot, practice the following:

Point the toe outward a small degree and take a short step backward and to the side, rolling the weight onto the flat foot. The knee must be relaxed as the weight is taken; at the same time, the upper body twists slightly over the standing foot. Quickly shift the weight back to the opposite foot to take a normal step on that foot. The body turns, at the same time, to face forward.

Practice the entire six counts of the foundation step, combining the footwork with the correct body action. Use a verbal count for a few repetitions; then recorded music.

The basic figure may turn in place. It is initiated by the toe of the leading foot being turned either inward or outward on the first count. The body follows the direction indicated by the placement of the toe until the dancer wishes to change the direction. Tell the students to develop the basic figure into a turning figure. Without partners, they must learn to turn both to the left and to the right. By making a strong, decisive step on the count of 1, with the toe of that foot pointed in the desired direction, they will find that it is easy to continue moving in the indicated direction.

The use of the arms is as important to Swing as proper footwork and body movements. To practice the use of the arm movements, ask the student to take partners.

Both partners extend their hands straight across to join hands with a finger clasp. The man holds his hands palm upward with fingers turned back toward himself; the lady holds her hands with palms facing downward and fingers turned back toward herself. The lady's fingers hook over those of the man's; he tightens the grasp to hold her fingers in a secure but flexible grip.

Both elbows of each dancer must be bent at an approximate right-angle and held fairly close to the dancer's own body. Controlled tension must be retained in the elbows and arms *at all times* to create a spring-like, elastic bond between the two dancers.

Temporarily, without regard to footwork being too exacting, practice the following use of the arms:

Dancers pull themselves together .... Slow
Dancers push partner backward to a normal
    standing position .... Slow
Push partners slightly backward, slightly
    beyond normal standing position .... Quick
Dancers draw partners forward to standing
    position .... Quick

During the practice interval, *both* partners must pull or push equally. Later, the man should be responsible for initiating the action, but the lady must cooperate by maintaining an equal amount of tension in her arms. If the tension in the arms is allowed to relax too much, the bond between the two dancers will be broken.

Finally, combine the feet, body, and arm actions into a coordinated, rhythmic sequence of movement. Practice the foundation pattern to count; then with music. Encourage the dancers to experiment with turning in place during the sequence of footwork. The turn is initiated, as in all dances, by the man making a definite, decisive turn of his foot in the direction he wishes to move. The turn may move either way, but it is never a rapid turn; it progresses by slow degrees in the desired direction.

DOUBLE LINDY

The Double Lindy figure is one in which the second count of the slow forward and backward steps is "filled in". There are several methods by which this may be accomplished. In all examples, men begin with *left* foot, ladies with right foot.

Example 1:

	Count
"Dig" the ball of the foot into the floor as the dancer steps forward	1
Bring *heel* of same foot down hard on floor	2
Step backward with opposite foot, "digging" ball of foot into floor	3
Bring *heel* of same foot down hard on floor	4

Counts 5 and 6 remain the same as in the Single Lindy figure.

Example 2:

	Count
Step forward on flat foot	1
Tap free foot beside standing foot	2
Step backward on flat foot	3
Tap free foot beside standing foot	4

(Note: the flat foot, the toe, or the heel may be used to make the *tap*)

Counts 5 and 6 remain same as in Single Lindy.

Example 3:

	Count
Swing leg forward and *tap* foot to floor	1
Step *in place* on same foot	2
Swing opposite leg backward and *tap* foot to floor	3
Step *in place* on same foot	4

Counts 5 and 6 remain same as in Single Lindy.

Practice all variations of the Double Lindy without turning; then with the turn.

As long as the basic rhythm of both partners is together, it is not necessary for them to be using identical footwork, that is, one may be using the Single Lindy while the other may be using a version of the Double Lindy.

With the development of skill and coordination, dancers may change from a two-hand hold to a one-hand hold. Any combinations may be used; right hands joined, left hands joined; left in right; or right in left. Students must practice changing handholds as they dance, timing the change to maintain the necessary spring-like tension in the arms.

BREAKAWAY VARIATION

Many figures may be learned to add variety and to give a different appearance to the basic footwork. One of these is the *Breakaway*. With a two-hand hold straight across, counts *1* through *4* are the same as either the Single Lindy or any choice of the Double Lindy. On count 5, the man pushes the lady backward with his *left* hand, causing her to step out to her right side. At the same time, he relaxes his *left* hand from her *right* hand, and he steps backward with his left foot. Momentarily, they are in a line, side by side (see illustration). On the count of *6*, the man quickly draws his partner toward him, using his *right* hand

which has retained the hold of her left hand. Because the action of the Breakaway figure is rapid, it is more comfortably used with slow or moderately-slow music.

With a little practice, the same action may be reversed to cause the figure to open to the opposite side.

UNDERARM CROSSOVER

A variety of turns may be used in Swing. The foundation footwork remains essentially the same as in the Single Lindy.

With the man holding the lady's *right* hand in his *right* hand, he raises their arms to make an arch. In effect, both dancers move forward to exchange places on the slow counts (cts. 1 through 4). At the same time, the man leads his partner *under* the arch formed by their arms so that she makes a complete turn to her right (clockwise). Counts 5 and 6 are the same as in the basic figure. In making the exchange of places, both partners need to remain close together. A quick adjustment of the finger hold must be made to facilitate the turn under the arch.

After the technique of the Underarm Turn has been practiced to a slow rhythm, *alternate* the figure with a basic Single Lindy in place. The combination of the two figures prevents the dancers from becoming dizzy.

Eventually, the turn may be made on the opposite side. For the change of sides the hand positions must be changed so that the man will be holding his partner's *left* hand in his *left* hand.

Skilled dancers frequently enjoy making the exchange of places on the *quick* counts, but students who have not gained sufficient dexterity and dance ability should not attempt it.

THE WALKAROUND

The *Walkaround* gives the dancers an opportunity to use an easy change of footwork from the basic figure. It is a series of short, staccato steps taken to correspond with each beat of the music. An even number of steps, such as six, eight, or ten, must be used to permit the dancers to return to the foundation figure with the proper foot. Any position may be used. For an easy beginning position, use a modified closed position in which dancers have their right sides adjacent. This is similar to the

"Swing" position in American square dancing. As the dancers turn in place using short, jabbing footwork accompanied by flexible knee action, they lean outward, pulling their shoulders away from their partner. After learning the figure with each partner moving forward, repeat it with both partners moving backward. If the dancers want to try the open position they stand side by side; one partner turns backward as the other moves forward. Ask the students to devise other positions and hand holds in which they use the Walkaround.

As a practice sequence, alternate one Single Lindy with eight counts of the Walkaround (in any position). All transitions must be made without hesitation or loss of rhythm.

TRIPLE LINDY

Advanced dancers who have become proficient in the Single Lindy and the Double Lindy enjoy adding the Triple Lindy to their repertory of Swing footwork. The figure involves the use of a "triplet", which is made in place of the slow counts. A triplet consists of three changes of weight made to two beats of music. The steps are short and fast, and are usually used to Swing music of a slow tempo.

As with other variations, men begin with the *left* foot, ladies with the *right* foot.

	Count
Short step *forward* on ball of foot	1
Close free foot to standing foot, changing weight	&
Short step *forward* on ball of foot	2
Short step *backward* on ball of foot	3
Close free foot to standing foot, changing weight	&
Short step *backward* on ball of foot	4

Counts 5 and 6 remain the same as in the Single Lindy figure.

Although young dancers usually prefer the freedom of movement made possible by using challenge position, they need to experience using the same footwork in the traditional closed position. Because of the closer body contact in ballroom position, the steps which were formerly used as either forward or backward movements become side to side movements. Closed

position is slightly more restrained, but the dance in closed position is equally as enjoyable and far more practical in crowded
dancing areas. (See illustration.)

Students need to practice combining all figures into combinations which are inventive and interesting. Single, Double and
Triple Lindy footwork may be mixed. As an example, the triplet
of the Triple Lindy may be used as the forward steps and the
step-hold of the Single Lindy may be tried on the backward
steps.

CHAPTER NINE

SAMBA
(Baión)

The *Samba*, as with many of the dances termed "Latin-American", owes its origin to the African natives who were brought to the new world in the early period of colonization. The Africans who had been transplanted to Brazil continued to sing their native songs and perform their African dances. With time, and the intermingling influences of Portuguese and other colonial cultures, both the songs and dances became interwoven into the permanent fabric of Brazilian lore.

In the days when Brazil was still a Portuguese empire, the tradition of Carnival began as a religious festival observed during the last three days before Lent. Ultimately, the religious significance of the occasion became secondary to one over which Momus, the ancient Greek monarch of satire and merry-making, held dominion. In the city of Rio de Janeiro, the festivals included pantomimes and plays ridiculing national figures as well as elaborate floats which depicted principal events of the year.

The feature which repeatedly drew the greatest attraction was provided by the Afro-Brazilians, most of whom lived in the poorer districts of the capital. Always dressed in original and imaginative costumes of their own devising, the Afro-Brazilians paraded, sang, and danced to the accompaniment of scintillating rhythms produced by an assortment of unique percussion instruments which included drums, rattles, and claves. The parades were not marched in the usual sense, but were danced in a jaunty, free-moving manner. At intervals, the paraders would stop and perform dances, some of which were of African origin.

One of the dances was the Batuqué (pronounced "Bah-too-KAY") in which the dancers formed a circle around a solo performer. As he finished his exhibition, the soloist chose a successor by gesturing toward one of the dancers in the circle and shouting, "Semba". The new dancer would then improvise a dance until he was ready to point out his chosen successor in the same manner. To the spectators, the shouted command, "Semba!", became the identifying mark of the dance. In the Portuguese language the pronunciation of the word altered from *Semba* to *Samba* (*a* as in *father*), the pronunciation also generally used in the United States.

In the 1920's, due to the overwhelming popularity of the American Fox Trot among Brazilian socialites, the characteristic steps and movements of the Carnival Samba were modified for use as a closed-position dance. The ballroom form of the dance retained the musical rhythms employed by the street dancers. As the ballroom Samba became increasingly popular, the custom became established of offering valuable prizes during Carnival for the most original musical compositions and songs in the Samba idiom.

The Brazilian Samba was introduced into the United States in 1935, but did not become widespread until about four years later. Failure to gain popular recognition was due, in part, to the required use of percussion instruments which were foreign to most musicians in the United States. The written music contained only the melodic line without musical notation for the accompanying percussion. In Brazil, and many other Latin-American countries, the musicians play the percussion accompaniment *ad libitum*, with variations suiting the skill and mood of the players. It was not until North American musicians learned to play the intricate percussion parts that the Samba became established as a familiar part of popular dance repertory.

STYLING   Although the dance is an exuberant one, it must be free of any uncontrolled jumping-back movements which develop into a contest of physical endurance. If danced correctly, the Samba can be smooth and controlled while still exuding the enthusiasm and joy typical of the dance.

The identifying characteristic of the Samba is the pendular swing of the dancer's bodies, mostly from the waist downward. The direction of the swing is usually forward and backward, but may also occasionally be used from side to side. As with most dances which show the influence of their African origins, the secret of performing it lies in the proper use of the pelvic muscles. In the Samba, the pelvic area serves as a "hinge" to separate the upper body from the legs. As the feet move forward the abdominal muscles contract, pulling the pelvis forward from the base of the spine. As the feet move backward the abdominal muscles release, permitting the pelvis to tip backward. The objective is to make the legs and feet swing forward and backward in a greater arc than that of the upper body. Although the gentle bouncing rhythm produced by the footwork must be permitted to carry upward into the shoulders and head, do not make a conscious effort toward tilting the upper body forward or backward. The head remains controlled as if a burden were being carried upon it which would be thrown off by any careless or inharmonious emphasis. The correct body movement of the Samba resembles, somewhat, that of a large bell suspended at the top by a yoke: the bottom swings in a generous arc while the top remains in one place. The sideward movement also results from relaxing the pelvic muscles to permit the tilting of the pelvis from side to side.

The footwork alternates, generally, from a step made on the flat of the foot to one taken on the ball of the opposite foot. The feet must remain close to the floor without being kicked forward or backward. The required springing action which must be permitted to carry upward through the body results from keeping the ankles and knees constantly loose and pliable.

Exaggerated arm movements characterized a part of the Samba when it was originally introduced to American dancers. Because these were too frequently used without imagination and with a total lack of development from natural movements, they became extremely mechanical and awkward. Set patterns of arm movements had never been used in Brazil, but had been borrowed from another dance, *the Maxixe* (pronounced "mahsheesh"), a Brazilian interpretation of the Polka typified by posturing arm movements and an overstated carriage of the head. The arms are *no longer* used in gestures which resemble railroad crossing semaphores or the reeling-in of a fishing line. Free, natural movements and gestures *should* be used to accent the body action as long as they emanate from the undulating motion of the body whenever the arms and hands are in a released position.

Although traveling figures are used in the dance, the Samba does not progress around the dancing area in the same manner as the Tango, Waltz, or Fox Trot. Samba dancers remain in a moderately limited area and perform free patterns of movement with, or around, their partners. The closed position was superimposed upon steps which were not meant to be inhibited by close contact. The majority of experienced Samba dancers prefer the freedom and variety which they obtain by alternately changing from closed position to one which is more open.

In recent years, a dance resembling the Samba, but using a more moderate tempo, has been introduced to the United States. In Brazil, the dance is termed the *Baión* (pronounced "buy-OWN"), but in the United States it is generally referred to as the "slow Samba". The Baión is written in 4/4 time, but the dance steps are counted in the same manner as the faster Samba. The mood of the Baión is of a more subdued, romantic nature than the faster Samba with its reflection of the Carnival spirit. The Baión requires greater control and skill to sustain the slower movements, but students who have gained sufficient mastery of the Samba will enjoy the experience presented in the slower dance.

RHYTHM ANALYSIS Sambas of moderate and fast tempo are written in 2/4 time, while the slow Samba, or the Baión, is composed in 4/4 time. In both dances, the footwork of the basic figures may be counted in multiples of two beats. A graphic diagram of two measures of 2/4 tempo may be illustrated in this manner:

2/4				
Count	1	&-2	1	&-2
Rhythm	S	Q-Q	S	Q-Q
Steps	L	R-L	R	L-R

The footwork alternates with every two beats of the music, that is, if the dancer begins with the *left* foot on the first measure, the second measure begins with the *right* foot, or the reverse procedure. *Three* changes of weight are made with the feet for each *two* beats of the music.

TEACHING PROGRESSIONS Listen to parts of several Samba recordings to permit the students to become familiar with the music. Accentuate the rhythm by counting aloud, and by using claves or other percussion instruments which blend with the music. Have the students indicate their understanding of the "1, &-2" rhythm by counting aloud or by clapping the metrical pattern. Because of the variety of percussion instruments used by Samba orchestras, students frequently require more time to learn to hear the basic rhythm than with music of a less complex structure.

After learning to distinguish and indicate the rhythm, move to the dancing area to begin the footwork. Unlike most dances, the Sambo boasts *two* basic figures; one which keeps the dancers in place, and the second which they use as a progressing or traveling figure. Both figures retain the same rhythm and styling, but the footwork in each of the two figures differs. Although some dance studios insist upon using the Portuguese names for the figures, the English translations are more practical for most instructors and students. These are: the *Bell* figure, which moves forward and backward in place (it is sometimes termed the "Pendulum"), and the *Samba Walk*, or *Samba Travel*, which is employed in progressing or traveling movements.

To practice the initial footwork, use the *Bell* figure; both men and women using the same footwork, without partners. Begin with a verbal count:

BELL FIGURE
(Also termed "Pendulum")

Steps	Count	Rhythm	Verbal Cue
Step fwd. on flat of LF	1	S	Flat
Step fwd. beside LF on ball of RF	&	Q	Toe
Step in place beside RF on flat of LF	2	Q	Flat

Step bkwd. on flat of RF	1	S	Flat
Step bkwd. beside RF on ball of LF	&	Q	Toe
Step in place beside LF on flat of RF	2	Q	Flat

Without regard to proper body motion, repeat the footwork gradually increasing the tempo of the counted rhythm. The dancer's feet must remain close to the floor but the action must not become a shuffling step. Keep both feet parallel during the forward and backward movement pointing the toes forward.

Repeat the action of the footwork of the Bell figure, requesting the students to keep their ankles and knees constantly relaxed to permit a natural "springy" action. Allow the gentle, bouncing rhythm to carry upward through the entire body. The body rhythm follows the slow-quick-quick pattern of the steps, and must be a controlled, vibrating motion which the dancer senses rather than being one which is too obvious.

With the aid of mental imagery, students will be able to understand the *contracting* and *releasing* action of the abdominal muscles which is a necessary part of Samba body action. Ask the students to think they are about to be struck in the abdomen by the fist of an imaginary person. The normal reaction should be one in which the abdominal muscles contract as a protective reflex. As the abdominal muscles contract they pull the pelvic bone forward from the base of the spine. As the muscles relax, the pelvic bone returns to its normal location, or, as happens in the completed figure, pulls backward by the contracted muscles at the back of the upper thigh.

Continue the experiment of gaining the *"contract and release"* action by having the students press against their abdominal muscles with their own hands. Extend the movements until the students become thoroughly aware of the action transpiring within their bodies. In the Samba, the pelvic area serves as a "hinge". By properly using the "hinge", the upper body of the dancer remains upright and controlled while the legs and feet are permitted to swing freely in pendular arcs.

Add the *"contract and release"* body action to the basic footwork. As the three steps are taken in a forward direction, the pelvic muscles must be contracted; as the steps are taken backward, the pelvic muscles are released permitting the muscles at the back of the thigh to pull the pelvis backward. The feet and legs must swing in a greater arc than that used by the upper body. Although the relaxed motion of the lower body extends upward, the dancers must not direct any conscious effort toward tilting the upper body forward or backward. Repeat the exercise with music, observing the correct timing of the footwork; that ankles and knees remain pliable; and that the *"contract and release"* action is properly coordinated without overdoing it.

After all the students have individually achieved the coordination of the proper body action and the footwork, permit them to practice the Bell Figure with a partner. The lady executes the exact counterpart of the man's steps.

For some students the shoulder-waist position (see section on Terminology) is more comfortable and easier to control than the traditional closed-position hold. Both positions are permissible in the Samba.

The Bell Figure may turn in place in either direction. The turn is initiated by leading with the toe turned in the desired direction on the count of 1. The feet constantly remain in a parallel position and fairly close together during the turning pattern. The degree of the turn must be small so that the dancers revolve slowly and with control in place.

SAMBA WALK
(or Samba Travel figure)

The second basic figure in the dance is the *Samba Walk*, and is used for progressing or traveling movements. The musical rhythm and the rhythmic motion produced in the body is the same as in the Bell Figure, but the footwork is not the same. The Samba Walk must *never be used in closed position*, but is used only in any open position in which each dancer faces the direction in which he wants to travel. The figure, Samba Walk, provides the greatest possibility for creative variations in the dance.

The Samba Walk uses the same *"contract and release"* movements described in the Bell Figure. The legs and feet also swing forward or backward in a greater arc than the head and shoulders, as in the Bell Figure. Although termed a "traveling" figure, it does not literally progress at a rapid rate of speed; all steps remain small and controlled. Because it is an exception to most dance footwork, caution the men against attempting to make their ladies move backward; the Samba Walk *only moves forward* for *both* men and women.

Because the footwork alternates, both men and women may practice the same footwork of the Samba Walk, without partners:

Steps	Count	Rhythm	Verbal Cue
Step fwd. on flat of LF, knee relaxed (The RF remains back in place, without weight upon it.)	1	S	Forward

Step bkwd. on toe of RF	&	Q	Back
Move the LF slightly bkwd. to step flat at a point about halfway between the space used for the first two changes of weight. (It is this count which causes the figure to progress.)	2	Q	Between
Reverse the entire action:			
Step fwd. on flat of RF, knee relaxed	1	S	Forward
Step bkwd. in place on toe of LF	&	Q	Back
Step halfway bkwd. on flat of RF	2	Q	Between

Practice the Samba Walk to a verbal count, gradually increasing the tempo as the dancers become familiar with the footwork. Practice the figure to recorded music; both men and women practicing without partners.

Arm movements are characteristically used with the Samba Walk whenever one or both hands are free. They must be the normal outgrowth of the natural body rhythm. In general, the arms swing forward and upward to about shoulder level on the count of 1; the action continues into a slight forward gesture of the forearm and hand on the count of &; the arm relaxes to about waist level on count 2. The arm movements alternate and follow the pattern of the feet, that is, the left arm moves forward as the left foot steps forward, or the same on the right side. Arm gestures should carry the movement into the shoulder so that each shoulder also moves slightly forward as the corresponding arm moves forward. All arm and shoulder movements need to be free and uninhibited, but not unnaturally extravagant.

After having been given time for each student to coordinate foot, body, and arm movements individually, each may take a partner to dance the Samba Walk. Initially, practice with dancers holding inside hands; outside hands and arms remain free to move with the body action. Both partners face the same direction for the first practice session. To music, let the dancers move around the dancing area any way they want to go.

To practice the Bell Figure and the Samba Walk, alternate six or eight measures of each figure. For the Bell Figure, use either shoulder-waist or closed position; for the Samba Walk, retain the same open position used during the practice of that figure. As the students gain in skill and experience, they may try the promenade position or any other open position with the Samba Walk.

During the practice combination, the instructor sees that the students maintain the same general character of body movement in both figures; that the dancers make the transition from one figure to another without losing rhythm. Encourage them to use the Bell Figure as a turning one.

INDIVIDUAL CIRCLES

In the *Individual Circle* figure each dancer travels, using the Samba Walk, in a small circular path *away* from his partner and around to *return* to his partner. Generally, the man's circle moves in a counterclockwise path; the lady's circle moves in a clockwise direction. The size of the circles depend upon the number of measures used to complete them. For practical purposes, six or eight measures are enough. The man directs his partner into the circle figure by gently pushing her away from him to her right as he begins his circle to his left. The free arms and hands must be used as in the previous Samba Walk exercises.

As a practice combination, alternate six measures of the Bell Figure with six measures of Individual Circles.

WHEEL TURN

In a *Wheel Turn* (see illustration), partners move around a central axis. This may be done with a variety of hand positions. For beginners, the most simple hold is one in which the man holds the lady's right hand in his right hand; both dancers face in opposite directions as they move in a small circle using the Samba Walk. After traveling the desired number of measures in one direction, partners turn toward one another to make a turn in place. Left hands are joined and the circle progresses in the opposite direction for the desired number of measures. Elbows of the joined arms may be bent to permit partners to remain close together; the free arm must move freely and naturally.

To practice the change of directions, begin with *right* hands joined to travel clockwise for six measures. On the sixth mea-

sure, partners release hands and turn *inward* toward each other to join *left* hands to move in the opposite direction, or counterclockwise. The circular path of movement does not need to be a complete, or literal, circle.

As with all figures using the Samba Walk, partners must begin with *opposite* feet; both partners must travel with the same rate of progress around their clasped hands serving as the axis of their circular direction. Make the inward turn on the sixth measure without altering the footwork, and without losing the rhythm.

Combine all of the Samba figures which have been practiced into the following temporary sequence:

Bell Figure	6 meas.
Samba Walk	6 meas.
Bell Figure	6 meas.
Individual Circles	6 meas.
Wheel Turn, *right* hands joined	6 meas.
Wheel Turn, *left* hands joined	6 meas.

Repeat the practice sequence until all dancers can manage the transitions smoothly and without losing rhythm. Observe that free arms are used in a relaxed manner and not held stiffly in place.

Request the students to *re-combine* the same figures in *any order* they desire, using as many measures as they wish for each figure. Urge the dancers to be imaginative and spontaneous and not to follow a set sequence of figures.

After the students have become thoroughly familiar and at ease with the basic figures of the Samba, they·will be ready to enjoy some of the more advanced figures:

COPACABANA WALK

The *Copacabana Walk* is an easy, but effective, variation of the Cuban Walk. Because the body swings from side to side, the Copacabana Walk must always be used in an open position, either with inside hands joined, or moving independently as in the Individual Circles (see illustration). The Copacabana Walk

lends professional styling to the Samba without being technically difficult.

For the Cuban Walk, the dancer steps straight forward on
the count of *1*, with the toe forward. For the Copacabana Walk,
the dancer turns the foot to point the toe *outward* on the count
of *1*, as he steps forward on that count. By turning the foot outward, the hips swing freely in the opposite direction, that is, if
the toe turns to the *left*, the hips normally twist to the *right*, or
the reverse procedure. By using opposite footwork, partners
alternately swing away and then together as they progress forward. The quick counts, *&-2*, remain essentially the same as in
the plain Cuban Walk and are made forward in the desired line
of direction. While dancing the Copacabana Walk, the free arms
swing in relaxed movements which grow out of the body motion.

SIDE PENDULUM

The Side Pendulum is similar to the Bell Figure, except that
the motion goes from side to side. The pelvic area needs to
retain the same relaxation typical of the other figures of the
Samba. The pelvic bone, in the Side Pendulum figure, tips from
side to side.

Practice the initial figure without partners, using the same
footwork for both men and women.

Steps	Count	Rhythm	Verbal Cue
Short step swd. on flat of LF	1	S	Side
Step behind LF on toe of RF	&	Q	Back
Step in place on flat of LF	2	Q	Place
Short step swd. on flat of RF	1	S	Side
Step behind LF on toe of RF	&	Q	Back
Step in place on flat of LF	2	Q	Place

After sufficient individual practice, dancers may take partners
in either closed or shoulder-waist position. The lady executes
the counterpart of the man's footwork, that is, as the man begins
with his left foot, the lady begins with her right foot, or the
reverse. For the initial practice, caution partners not to twist
their bodies as they bring the foot in back of the standing foot.
They will gain more control by keeping their hips and shoulders

parallel as the feet swing from side to side. As more experience
and skill is accomplished, the Side Pendulum may be danced
with a more amplified twisting motion of the bodies, if desired.

To practice the Side Pendulum in combination with other
figures, use the following sequence:

Bell Figure .... 4 meas.
Side Pendulum .... 4 meas.
Samba Walk .... 4 meas.
Side Pendulum .... 4 meas.

Repeat the practice combination until all figures flow together
without difficulty.

Tell the students to create their own free-style routine by
adding the Copacabana Walk and the Side Pendulum to their
repertory of Samba figures. Observe that they use arm movements as well as correct footwork.

Encourage the students to experiment in developing original
patterns of movement or to alter the usual appearance of a
figure by trying different hand positions. Examples: (1) Man
dances in place using the basic Bell Figure as he leads his partner in a circle around himself. The lady uses either the Samba
Walk or the Copacabana Walk to progress slowly around him.

(2) Assume Varsovienne position (see section on Terminology)
for the Cuban Walk figure (partners must continue to use opposite footwork).

SAMBA SQUARE

In most dances, the Square or Box figure is frequently the
foundation figure. In the Samba, however, the Square figure is a
more advanced one which should not be introduced until the
dancers gain enough control and experience to perform it without becoming confused. The footwork basically resembles a
Waltz Square, but the quicker, uneven tempo develops a counter motion in the upper body which can unnerve an unwary
beginner.

The *Samba Square* may be performed in either the traditional
closed position or in shoulder-waist position. Ankles, knees, and
pelvic area must remain pliable.

Directions are for the man; the lady dances the counterpart.

Steps	Rhythm
Step fwd. on flat of LF	S
Short step swd. on toe of RF	Q
Close LF to RF on flat of LF	Q
Step bkwd. on flat of RF	S
Short step swd. on toe of LF	Q
Close RF to LF on flat of RF	Q

The figure may also turn in place, in either direction. Initiate the turn in the same manner as a Waltz Square.

CHAPTER TEN

FOX TROT

BACKGROUND His name did not appear on the marquee of the theatre in which he was performing, yet Harry Fox unkowingly contributed his name to a dance that was to become an international favorite. Harry Fox, a personable young vaudevillian and musician, embellished his act in one of New York's musical shows of the 1913 season by alternately playing ragtime rhythms on the piano and dancing around the stage with each of several attractive girls who formed part of the living decor. The popular dances of the era consisted of frenetic exercises grotesquely performed to "ragtime" rhythm which had overwhelmed the dancing public with its syncopated appeal. The dances, many of them reputed to have originated in San Francisco's Barbary Coast and New York's Bowery, bore descriptive names such as *Grizzly Bear, Turkey Trot, Bunny Hug, Kangaroo Hop,* and the *Harem Glide.*

The "trot" performed by Harry Fox and his bevy of chorines presented a new challenge and novelty to that part of the dancing public with the insatiable urge to be part of the latest trend. Urgent demands to learn the new dance were voiced. Dancing teachers were quick to respond to the requests and the stage version of the *Fox Trot* was modified to meet the needs of the ballroom. The dance soon replaced all others in popularity, but remained essentially a spontaneous "trot" performed with the exaggerated body bounce and accompanied by the effusive pumping movements of the arms that had been a typical part of the other dances inspired by the scintillating, syncopated ragtime rhythms. Afternoon tea dances or "thés dansants", had become established earlier in the fashionable hotels and clubs in

125

most of the major cities. With the introduction of the Fox Trot, the afternoon dances extended into the evenings to become "diner dansants", and in some instances, evolved into "breakfast dansants".

When the United States became actively aligned in World War I, dancing served as both a tension-reliever and an escape from unpleasant news bulletins. American doughboys, on leave from front line trenches, eased war-strained nerves and abated attacks of homesickness by teaching the Fox Trot to the "mademoiselles from gay Paree".

After World War I, the trend in popular music slowly changed from the old ragtime to a smoother blues rhythm, to which the Fox Trot readily adapted. The body bounce became more controlled and the "trotting" footwork grew into gliding movements to match the mellow mood of the saxophone, which had gained a predominant role in every popular orchestra.

Throughout the 1930's, which were years of financial depression, stock market crashes, and bank failures, the popular public recreation remained ballroom dancing, and the Fox Trot continued as the favorite. Public and private ballrooms flourished, and the services of dance orchestras under the direction of prominent leaders were in eager demand. The musical form of the Fox Trot again changed into one with a more melodic and smooth character. The dance shed all traces of the original "trotting" steps and the movements became smoothly controlled with gliding footwork.

The Fox Trot of today is a graceful dance with only a most subtle body movement to correspond with the syncopation of the musical rhythm. In company with the Waltz, the Fox Trot has become an almost universal dance and is a favorite throughout the world wherever people perform ballroom dancing.

The Fox Trot is a comparatively foolproof dance to a person who has gained some knowledge of rhythm and basic movements. Its seeming simplicity is deceptive, however, and it is not a good one to be taught as the initial dance to beginning students. The dance comes alive only when the two basic figures in its composition are combined in a free and imaginative manner to correspond with the vast variety of moods and traits expressed by Fox Trot music. Beginning dancers are not able to cope with improvization and free movement which the Fox Trot demands. To practice to a set routine is not only dull and stilted, but is also a limiting experience for the student. A routine set to one selection of Fox Trot music rarely fits any other selection. For these reasons, it is wise to delay the teaching of the Fox Trot until the problems presented in leading, following, and improvizing have become more familiar and the student can use them with a degree of satisfaction.

STYLING   The Fox Trot starts with the same closed ballroom position used in the Waltz; Promenade and Open positions may be injected at times to lend variety. Both dancers need to maintain good posture but their bodies must be relaxed. The combination of quick and slow steps needs to be smoothly blended and not performed in a halting, uncertain manner. All steps are taken with the *Dancer's Walk*, that is, the toe of the foot touches the floor before the heel is put down. The free foot "follows through" by being brought near the standing foot, almost touching it, as a step is made either forward or backward. On the slow counts, the free foot is brought to the standing foot without a transfer of weight. In all footwork, the feet remain close to the floor and appear to glide across the floor. Generally, leg movements originate from the hips and not from the knees. As steps are made, the weight remains on the forward ball of the foot; rarely is the heel brought down heavily upon the floor.

RHYTHM ANALYSIS   Fox Trot music is written in 4/4 time, indicating four beats to each measure. Each beat receives the same amount of time, but there are a variety of methods used in placing the accent to achieve the effect and quality desired by the musical arranger. In some Fox Trot music, only the first beat in each measure is accented; in others, both the first and third receive equal stress; in the more contemporary "swing" styling, the accents shift to the second and fourth beats. In all usage, however, the accents in the music are smooth and harmonious but stimulating enough to hold the interest of dancers. Generally, dancers follow the same accents established in the music.

The Fox Trot dancer needs to create an interesting and spontaneous pattern from the two basic rhythms used in the footwork. These are *slow* steps and *quick* steps which may be combined with endless variety. The *slow* steps require *two* beats of music, while the *quick* steps require *one* beat. The *quick* steps may be combined in any multiple of *two*. In using a series of *slow* steps, dancers add the syncopation of the second beat by slightly bending the knee of the standing foot on the second count.

The following graphic diagrams compare the *quick* and *slow* rhythms in a two-measure unit:

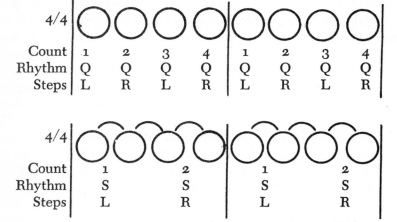

4/4								
Count	1	2	3	4	1	2	3	4
Rhythm	Q	Q	Q	Q	Q	Q	Q	Q
Steps	L	R	L	R	L	R	L	R

4/4				
Count	1	2	1	2
Rhythm	S	S	S	S
Steps	L	R	L	R

Any combination of *slow* and *quick* (in multiples of two) steps may be made.

TEACHING PROGRESSIONS   Listen to parts of several selections of slow, moderate and fast Fox Trot music, paying special attention to the "beat" established by the base and percussion instruments. Assist the students in counting a series of *quick* beats; then a series of *slow* beats. The *slow* rhythm, which is a combination of two *quick* beats, may be counted as: 1 &, 2 &, 3 &,. Make certain that the students sense the syncopation which takes place on the "&" count, or the *second half* of the *slow* beat.

When the students gain a sufficient understanding of the musical rhythm, they then translate the intellectual knowledge of the music into physical action.

Begin by using the *quick* rhythm, taking one step on each *quick* beat. After "walking" the steps for enough measures to permit the students to synchronize the movement with the musical rhythm, add the correct styling of the "dance walk" to the footwork. The rule of the *toe* of the foot touching the floor before the heel applies for movements taken forward or those taken backward. The dancers' feet remain close to the floor, generally, but the steps must not become a shuffling movement; rather they must maintain a light-stepping quality.

Without partners, practice the *quick* steps moving forward for a few measures, then moving backward.

A syncopated movement in the body that is not used in the *quick* movements characterizes the *slow* movements of the Fox Trot, especially whenever they are used in a series. The syncopation is gained by a subtle bending of the knee on the second part of the *slow* step, which is a combination of two *quick* counts. The bending of the knee must not be overdone, or even obvious, but the dancer must be aware of the movement.

Practice a series of *slow* steps by having the students, without partners, move around the dancing area to a *counted* "step-bend, step-bend" rhythm with all students moving forward; repeat, with all students moving backward. As with the *quick* steps, the *toe* of the leading foot must touch the floor before the heel is brought down. Repeat the *slow* exercise using music of a moderate tempo.

With partners, have the students parctice a series of *quick* and a series of *slow* steps, changing directions by having the men move forward, and then backward. Use Fox Trot music of a moderate tempo.

If the students have sufficient skill, let them practice the following exercises with partners. The instructor should verbally count each rhythm for a few measures before using recorded music.

Combine *two* slow steps with *two* quick steps; practice moving forward and backward.

Combine *three* slow steps with *two* quick steps. In this combination, the footwork alternates from side to side, that is, if the dancer begins the series with the *left* foot, he starts the subsequent series with the *right* foot. Practice moving forward and backward.

Request the students to practice to music, either with or with-

out partners, *any combination* of slow and quick steps which the
music dictates. Men with partners need to be encouraged to
communicate the change of rhythms to their partners with
strong definite leading movements of their hands.

The instructor must observe that the students use the "dance
walk"; that their feet "follow through", that is, the free foot
passes close to the standing foot in moving forward or backward,
and not in a wide, "straddle" position; and that the dancers
maintain a controlled but not stiff, erect posture.

Because some dancers find it difficult to improvise in a creative manner, we have selected several traditional combinations
which help the beginning Fox Trot dancers.

BASIC FIGURE

Although authorities disagree as to which combination should
be termed the "basic" one in the Fox Trot, this one is valuable
because it alternates footwork.

Steps	Count	Rhythm
Step fwd. on LF	1-2	S
Step fwd. on RF	3-4	S
Short step fwd. on LF	5	Q
Short step fwd. on RF	6	Q
Step fwd. on LF	7-8	S
Step fwd. on RF	1-2	S
Step fwd. on LF	3-4	S
Short step fwd. on RF	5	Q
Short step fwd. on LF	6	Q
Step fwd. on RF	7-8	S

Without partners, briefly practice the "basic figure moving
forward; then reverse the footwork to move backward.

Repeat the same exercise with partners, the lady using the
counterpart of the man's steps.

An interesting "twinkle" variation may be developed from the
"basic" figure by making a change of direction on the quick
steps. Use it in this manner:

Steps	Count	Rhythm
Step fwd. on LF	1-2	S
Step fwd. on RF	3-4	S

Short step fwd. on LF	5	Q
Close RF to LF, *changing weight*	6	Q
Step *bkwd.* on LF	7-8	S
Step bkwd. on RF	1-2	S
Step bkwd. on LF	3-4	S
Short step bkwd. on RF	5	Q
Close LF to RF, *changing weight*	6	Q
Step *fwd.* on RF	7-8	S

In closed position, the lady uses the counterpart of the man's steps.

BOX STEP

While other methods may be taught to form a Box, or Square figure in the Fox Trot, the most popular combination consists of two quick steps and one slow step, in this manner:

Steps	*Count*	*Rhythm*
Short step swd. on LF	1	Q
Close RF to LF, *changing weight*	2	Q
Step fwd. on LF	3-4	S
Short step swd. on RF	1	Q
Close LF to RF, *changing weight*	2	Q
Step bkwd. on RF	3-4	S

The lady uses the counterpart to the man's footwork in closed position.

One may develop the Box figure into a turning figure with quarter-turns; or a progressive traveling figure by using half-turns. The technique is the same as that used in making the Waltz turns, except that the rhythm in the Fox Trot turn will be "quick-quick, slow" instead of the even counts of the Waltz.

ANGLE TWO-STEP

The two-step was one of the basic figures of the original Fox Trot. This figure may still be used as part of the Fox Trot, but more advanced dancers frequently use a slightly altered form in which they make the first step on a diagonal to the line of travel. In closed position, the lady uses the counterpart of the man's footwork.

Steps	*Count*	*Rhythm*
Short step diag. swd. on LF (toe of LF is turned slightly inward, at same time, body turns slightly to right)	1	Q
Close RF to LF, *changing weight* (body remains slightly to right)	2	Q
Step fwd. in LOD on LF (at same time, turning body slightly to left to face LOD)	3-4	S
Short step diag. swd. on RF (toe of RF turned slightly inward, at same time, body turns slightly to left)	1	Q
Close LF to RF, *changing weight* (body remains slightly to left)	2	Q
Step fwd. in LOD on RF (at same time, turning body slightly to right to face LOD)	3-4	S

The quick diagonal steps produce a slight sideward swing in the dancers' bodies. It is easy to make a transition from, or into, the Box figure from the Angle Two-Step. Both are similar in rhythm and technique.

An infinite variety of combinations may be achieved by combining *slow* and the *quick* steps to Fox Trot rhythm. Encourage the students to experiment in creating their own patterns. While the general direction of movement in the Fox Trot is in a counterclockwise line around the dancing area, simple changes such as zig-zag movements or movements in a small circle create the illusion of a different figure without actually altering the basic footwork. The Fox Trot requires an element of jauntiness, but all footwork and body rhythm should be harmoniously blended into a varied but relaxed whole. The simplicity and relaxation with which it may be used permits Fox Trotters the pleasure of dancing for many hours without undue fatigue or strain.

CHAPTER ELEVEN

AMERICAN RUMBA

BACKGROUND   A dance termed the Rumba was presented to North American ballroom enthusiasts in 1930. Although the introduction was given by someone who had ostensibly made a study of the dances of Cuba, the researcher failed to identify it properly and presented another one under the misconception that it was the Rumba. The genuine Rumba is a pantomimic exhibition dance, performed by professional dancers who depict aspects of life in the rural areas of Cuba. While it is traditionally performed by a man and a woman, they dance separately, each acting out their story as the other waits his turn in the background.

The dance so mistakenly identified as the Rumba is actually the Cuban Son (pronounced with a long "o"), a social dance in traditional ballroom form. The underlying rhythm of both the Rumba and the Son are similar, but the Rumba is played at a faster tempo. There is an entire group of Cuban dances which have similar rhythms and can be traced to the religious and ceremonial dances of Africa. When African slaves were unwillingly transported to Cuba by the earliest blackbirders, they carried their forms of music and dance with them. While contact with a popourri of other cultures and races has altered the dance forms, the basic African rhythm remains almost unchanged.

The old African instruments are still played in the same manner used in their native land. They consist of a variety of drums, gourds, bamboo and hardwood sticks, rattles and gongs which are struck, shaken, or scratched to produce percussive sounds. One instrument is frequently played at a rhythmic counterpoint to another. To persons unfamiliar with music of this character, the differences are frequently too subtle to distinguish. Because they are so easily confused, in the United States several Cuban

133

dances which share similar musical cadences have been grouped
together under the common heading of "American Rumba".

Among these are: the *Son*, played at a moderate tempo in a
staccato manner. The *Guaracha*, distinguished by its fast, bright,
and cheerful tempo. The *Cuban Bolero* is smooth and slow, and
carries a definite resemblance to African tribal 'rhythms. The
Mambo developed by adding a syncopated, or jazz, beat to the
true Rumba rhythm. The *Cha-Cha* developed from one figure
used in the Mambo. These, and a few lesser known dances,
make up the "Rumba family". Most of the dances share a box,
or square, figure in the footwork. The figure has come to be
known as the "Rumba Box", and is the foundation of the American Rumba.

While professional dance studios find it to their advantage
to distinguish between each of the dances in their advanced
classes, the usual high school or college student in a beginning
class will find it sufficiently challenging to master the one version inclusively defined as "American Rumba".

Almost any recording marked either *Rumba, Bolero, Guaracha,* or *Son* is suitable for American Rumba, allowing for the
necessary adaptation to the tempo and mood of each selection.

STYLING   The footwork and figures of the American Rumba are
not difficult, but without the proper body movement, which has
been borrowed from the Afro-Cuban dancers, the dance becomes negative and uninteresting. The movement which gives
the dance its distinguishing characteristic is the result of *allowing* the sheath of muscles girdling the middle body to *relax*
enough to permit the pelvis to tilt as the weight of the body
transfers from one foot to the other. It is a normal action which
has been experienced by everyone at some time. It frequently
occurs when a person is required to stand in one place for a
period of time such as waiting for a bus, remaining in a slow-
moving queue, or standing and talking with a friend. The same
pelvic movement, so frequently made unconsciously, is the key
to the hip action required in the American Rumba.

The error commonly made by dancers in the United States is

to attempt to *initiate* the action from the hips rather than letting it result from shifting the body weight from foot to foot while the ankles, knees, and pelvis are all properly "at ease". The hip shifts as a *result* of stepping upon one foot and letting the hip follow with a slightly delayed timing. Although the pelvic muscles must be relaxed, they must not sag. The shifting of weight from foot to foot and the resultant hip action must all be employed in a buoyant, effortless manner.

The relaxed rhythm carries upward through the spinal column into the shoulder and neck muscles which remain controlled without obvious action. Anthropologists state that the characteristic Rumba body action is a natural one to people who carry burdens upon their heads, frequently walking barefoot over rough terrain. Any antagonistic movement of the head causes the burden to fall.

In dancing the Rumba, keep all steps very small, not more than four or five inches in length. Any large step taken sideward, forward, or backward automatically locks the muscles and joints in the bridge-like arch formed by the pelvis and the supporting leg bones.

When the Rumba was originally introduced into the United States an exotic, affected hand hold was assumed. This is no longer used and the closed position is the same one used in Waltz, Tango, or Fox Trot. The closed position, however, is one that was superimposed upon older patterns of footwork that were not meant to be inhibited by close contact with a partner. More skillful Rumba dancers prefer to limit their use of the closed position in favor of the open, freer, positions.

The Rumba, both the Cuban and American versions, does not progress around the dancing area as does the Waltz or Tango, but remains in a small area. The man leads his partner around him, or he dances around her in an endless pattern of slow movements. The dance does not need an elaborate sequence of figures, but needs to be danced with sincerity. The dancer's feet should remain close to the floor but are picked up and put down on each step, never shuffled across the floor. The footwork should have an "earthy" quality with the full foot taking the weight on each step.

RHYTHM ANALYSIS   American Rumba music may be written in either 2/4 or 4/4 time. In either case the basic rhythm may be computed in counts of *four*. Each count, or beat, is of equal duration.

A graphic diagram of two measures of Rumba rhythm can be illustrated in this manner:

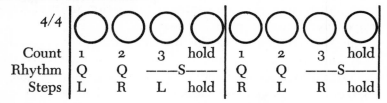

4/4	1	2	3	hold	1	2	3	hold
Count	1	2	3	hold	1	2	3	hold
Rhythm	Q	Q	----S----		Q	Q	----S----	
Steps	L	R	L	hold	R	L	R	hold

While the rhythm may be counted "quick-quick, slow", to indicate that counts 3 and 4 combine into one long count, beginning students have a better understanding of the rhythm when the count, "1, 2, 3, hold" is called. This count corresponds with the changes of weight in the foot pattern. Claves or other percussion instruments may be used by the instructor to emphasize the basic "1, 2, 3, hold" rhythm.

TEACHING PROGRESSIONS   For beginning students, the correct rhythm is often difficult to distinguish in Rumba music. The perplexity stems from the involved use of percussion instruments in the base section of the orchestra. In the hands of experienced musicians, these instruments are frequently played in rhythms counter to one another and produce a polyphonic sound challenging to analyze.

Because most musicians trained in the United States are not as adept at using the unfamiliar percussion instruments, the rhythm in their recordings is not as complex and difficult to find. For this reason, it is recommended that beginning dancers be introduced to the American Rumba by using recordings made by North American artists. Later, after they have learned to hear and to "feel" the rhythm, they will find the music of the true Latin orchestra exciting and appealing.

After listening to enough recordings to become familiar with the rhythm of the American Rumba, the students may begin to learn the footwork with its accompanying body movement.

Standing in a position with the feet not more than four or five inches apart, and with the muscles around the pelvic area as relaxed as is comfortably possible, slowly transfer the entire body weight to the left leg and foot, including the heel. The left knee, while straight enough to support the body weight, should *not* be drawn backward into a tightly locked position, but must remain semi-relaxed. In this position, if the right knee and right hip are properly relaxed, the left hip should have made a small movement toward the left and should be slightly higher than the right hip. Slowly shift the body weight over the right leg and foot, including the heel, and note that the reverse movement has taken place.

Repeat the exercise slowly with the students holding their hands on their hips to experience the sideward movement of the pelvis. All transfers of weight need to be fluid and smoothly controlled to produce an elastic, rolling quality.

The action should be allowed to flow upward into the rib cage and along the spine but the upper body and shoulders must remain controlled without any large, counteracting motions being obvious.

To a verbal count, or with a percussion instrument, and with the students remaining in place, repeat the exercise to the basic "1, 2, 3, hold" rhythm. Although there is no change of weight on the 4th count, the hip movement does continue through that beat. This is accomplished by the dancer *anticipating* the change of weight and starting the movement of the hip to the side *in preparation* to placing the weight on the foot on the following count of 1.

Footwork, hips, musical counts and rhythms are always synchronized in this manner:

Weight on Foot	Hip swings to	Musical Count	Rhythm
LF	left	1	Q
RF	right	2	Q
LF	left	3	
hold	begins swing to right	4	S
RF	right	1	Q
LF	left	2	Q
RF	right	3	
hold	begins swing to left	4	S

The sideward movements of the hip on each count are constant and will not be indicated in the directions which follow. It is vital that all steps be kept short and made with a controlled rolling change of weight from foot to foot.

RUMBA BOX, or SQUARE

The Rumba Box, or Square, is similar to figures used in many dances. The Rumba Box preferably begins with a sideward step. With the students working individually, practice the figure to count, then with music.

Steps	Count	Verbal Cue
Short step swd. on LF	1	Side,
Close RF to LF, changing wt.	2	close,
Short step fwd. on LF	3	forward,
Hold in place		hold.
Short step swd. on RF	1	Side,
Close LF to RF, changing wt.	2	close,
Short step bkwd. on RF	3	back,
Hold in place	4	hold.

The Box figure may be developed into a turning one by leading with the toe turned either outward or inward on the first count and continuing to move in the direction indicated by that first step. All turning figures in the Rumba should be made slowly, taking four measures or more to make one complete revolution.

The Rumba Box may begin in the reverse order from that notated, that is, the footwork could be: "RF to side, close, step back; LF to side, close, step forward".

After working individually on the Rumba Box, both without turning and with the turn, ask the students to take partners and repeat the same figures in closed position. The lady uses the counter step to that of the man.

CUBAN WALK

The traveling sequence used in the Rumba is known as the *Cuban Walk*. It may be used in any direction, traveling forward, backward, or in circles. Closed, promenade, or any open position may be used. All steps must be short and performed without any feeling of having to move with urgency or haste. They must not be permitted to deteriorate into a shuffle. Ankles, knees, and hips must remain relaxed and employed in the same manner used in the Rumba Box.

Initially, practice the traveling figure without partners, both men and women using the same footwork.

Steps	Count
Short step fwd. on LF	1
Short step fwd. on RF	2
Short step fwd. on LF	3
Hold weight on LF (Free foot may be touched to floor beside standing foot without any transfer of weight.)	4
Short step fwd. on RF	1
Short step fwd. on LF	2
Short step fwd. on LF	3
Hold weight on RF (Free foot beside standing foot, as above.)	4

Continue to practice Cuban Walk forward for several measures, observing that the styling and timing are in the desired Rumba character. In the Cuban Walk, one or both arms are frequently in a free position. They should move in a natural counter-rhythm dictated by the foot and body movements. Any attempt to use the arms in exaggerated gestures, or to force them into set patterns is contrary to good Rumba styling.

Reverse the figure with both men and women moving backwards in the Cuban Walk.

Practice the Cuban Walk with partners in closed position, men moving forward; reverse the figure with men moving backward. Practice the Walk in promenade or in open position with both partners moving forward; then backward. (In promenade or in open position, both partners must have their weight on opposite feet.)

As an aid to making an effortless transition from one figure to another, have the students dance the following practice combination.

Rumba Box in place	4 meas.
Cuban Walk, men moving fwd.	4 meas.

Rumba Box in place	4 meas.
Cuban Walk, men moving bkwd.	4 meas.

After sufficient practice, repeat a similar combination developing the Rumba Box figures into a left turn (counterclockwise) in place for 4 measures.

With couples remaining in closed position, practice the following sequence in which dancers use an *odd* number of Cuban Walk figures:

Rumba Box turning left (CCW), man beginning with LF	4 meas.
Cuban Walk, man moving fwd. beginning with LF	5 meas.
Rumba Box turning right (CW), man beginning with RF and stepping *back* on ct. 3	4 meas.
Cuban Walk, man beginning RF to move backward	5 meas.

Practice the exercise until the changes of direction in both figures can be accomplished smoothly. It is not necessary for the dancers to make a complete turn in place with the Rhumba Box figure.

Let the students create their own combination alternating the Rumba Box with the Cuban Walk. At the same time, they should practice varying the position, moving from a closed position to a promenade or other more open position. Any number of measures may be used for each figure. Encourage the students to be inventive and original in their patterns as long as the limitations of styling and rhythm are observed. This, essentially, *is* the American Rumba which, like its Cuban parent, should never be danced in a set sequence of figures. Rumba music usually projects an exciting, carnival-like spirit which should be reflected in the dancers. If they are having fun, they should show it!

While it is easy enough to request dancers to "be inventive", very few will undertake to depart from the basic patterns used in the practice sequences. For their benefit, several additional figures have been listed which are typical to Rumba, and use the same body movements and rhythm.

UNDERARM TURNS

From closed position, the man marks time in place (LF, RF, LF, hold; etc.) as he directs his partner under their clasped arms (his left, her right). The lady begins with her right foot, using the Cuban Walk, to make a very small, slow turn in place. Her steps should be small, requiring about *four* measures to make the complete revolution.

The figure may reverse with the man turning under their clasped arms as the lady marks time in place.

Both partners may turn under the arch at the same time, the lady turning right (CW), the man turning left (CCW). During this figure, both partners must remain close together, bodies almost touching, as they revolve in place.

The entire sequence may be used *without* hands being held, if the dancers desire. The man, however, should be responsible for directing his partner into the turns he wishes her to use.

WHEEL TURNS

Wheel Turns are those in which partners turn about an imaginary axis that is common to both.

From closed position, while retaining the closed position hand hold, the man steps to his left to bring the right side of his body adjacent to the right side of his partner. With Cuban Walk steps, they both walk forward, turning in a clockwise circle, for any desired number of measures. To change the direction of the circle, dancers slowly turn toward their partners while continuing to use Cuban Walk steps, to bring the left sides of their bodies together. It is not necessary to change the hand hold. The dancers again move forward to make a counterclockwise circle. The figure may also be executed with partners moving *backwards* to circle in place.

The same circular direction of movement may be accomplished by the use of other hand positions. With partners facing in opposite directions but standing in a line side by side, they join inside hands (lady's right in man's right hand). Arms are held slightly upward with elbows bent at an angle to bring partners together (see illustration in chapter on Samba). The free hands of both dancers should be relaxed to move in any natural manner which corresponds with the rhythm of their bodies. To make a change in the direction of the circle, dancers release clasped hands and slowly turn toward their partner to join the other hands.

Encourage students to explore other methods of using the Wheel Turn figure.

RUMBA DOS-A-DOS

The Cuban Walk is used for this figure which is similar to to one used in American Square Dancing. It is a favorite one of most young dancers.

With partners facing, they advance to pass right shoulders. Without turning around, they each move sideward to pass back-to-back and return, moving backwards to pass left shoulders, to their original places. It is not necessary to use any specific number of measures to complete the figure.

Dancers need to be encouraged to experiment with making other patterns of movement around their partners. Various hand holds should accompany some of the figures.

As each figure of the Rumba is taught, the teacher should combine it with one or two other figures which the students have learned previously. The objective should be to achieve a smooth blending of the figures without loss of the characteristic Rumba rhythm and styling.

In Rumba, when music of a fast tempo is used, the dancers' footwork needs to be proportionately *smaller* to compensate for the increased speed. Most dancers make the error of attempting to increase the size of their steps. At times, the action taking place within the dancer's body may be "fast and furious", but a good Rumba dancer retains complete command of the action and does not permit it to become frenetic and frenzied.

As is true with other dances, a Rumba dancer need not know an endless number of figures but must be able to combine the ones he does know with deftness and imagination.

SUGGESTED DANCE REFERENCES

Numerous excellent books have been written about the many facets of dance, of which popular dance is only one. Because all dancing has an inter-relationship, an instructor of popular dancing should strive to broaden his scope by exploring the writings of authorities who have contributed to the full spectrum of the art rather than those limited specifically to popular dancing.

Some of the suggested books are no longer currently in print but may be obtained from school or public libraries. Many may be purchased from used book sources.

The references are not listed in any order of specific importance: *Frederick Rand Rogers,* editor, DANCE: A BASIC EDUCATIONAL TECHNIQUE, MacMillan Company, 1941. An outstanding anthology of material from many illustrious dancers and dance educators. Although generally directed toward other forms of dancing, the material can easily be applied to the instruction and performance of popular dance. The section devoted to body development and control should be studied by all dance instructors.

Earl Leaf, ISLES OF RHYTHM, A. S. Barnes and Company, 1948. Mr. Leaf, a photographer, has captured in both the written word and by photography, a most remarkable history-story record of the peoples of the Caribbean islands with their dances, religious customs, and folkloric arts. It is from these islands that we derive most of the dances we so loosely classify as "Latin-American"

Veloz and Yolanda, TANGO AND RUMBA, Harper & Brothers, 1938. The authors were recognized as the most outstanding team of exhibition ballroom dancers in the United States during the era in which the book was published. Although some of the material has become dated, much is still useable. Their chapter on "Form and Finish" contains many suggestions as current today as when the book was published.

Betty White, BALLROOM DANCING FOR TEACHERS (1962); DANCING MADE EASY (1958); LATIN-AMERICAN DANCE-BOOK (1958); TEEN-AGE DANCE BOOK (1952); and others, David McKay Company, Inc., Publishers. A remarkable collection of current material on popular dancing enhanced by diagrams and illustrations. Several books contain additional material on party games, mixers, and dance etiquette.

Curt Sachs, WORLD HISTORY OF THE DANCE, W. W. Norton & Company, 1937. The most comprehensive history available in English of all forms of dancing from the stone age to contemporary times.

La Meri (Russell Meriweather Hughes), DANCE AS AN ART FORM, A. S. Barnes & Company, 1933. An interesting preliminary volume of study for both the serious student and instructor. It covers many facets of dancing with their backgrounds and histories. The "Table of Dances" outlining the country, form, and origin of more than 100 dances is useful as in the glossary.

Anita and Dexter Wright, HOW TO DANCE, Garden City Publishing Company, 1942 with several later revisions. The authors have been teachers and authorities of popular dancing from the days of the Turkey Trot to the present. The earliest editions of the book contain dances no longer in popular use but which will be of interest to dance historians. These dances include the Conga, Lambeth Walk, and Shag.

Anatol Chujoy, DANCE ENCYCLOPEDIA, A. S. Barnes and Company, 1949. An exciting almanac for enthusiasts of all aspects of dancing from ancient to modern times. Contains biographies of well-known dancers as well as informative articles by several dance authorities.

Walter Sorell, editor, THE DANCE HAS MANY FACES, World Publishing Company, 1951. Twenty-nine authorities on "the many faces of dance" and related subjects have contributed to a valuable and comprehensive symposium.

Irene and Vernon Castle, MODERN DANCING, Harper & Brothers, 1914. The Castles were the outstanding exponents of popular ballroom dancing in the 1914-18 era. They were responsible for introducing the smoother, more sophisticated element of dance styling to the ballroom that is still desirable as a standard in popular dancing. Although the dances described in the book have long ago been replaced, they should have an historic appeal to the serious educator of popular dancing.

Irene Castle, CASTLES IN THE AIR, Doubleday & Company, 1958. A biography of Irene Castle, who, with Vernon Castle, changed the dancing habits of American dancers. The references to the popular dances used in the early part of this century should be of interest to students and teachers of popular dancing.

Marshall W. Stearns, THE STORY OF JAZZ, Oxford University Press, New York City, 1956. Includes history, theory, biographies and references to Jazz music and musicians. A section on Afro-Cuban music and dance makes it especially valuable to the teacher of Latin-American dances.

Margaret N. H'Doubler, DANCE: A CREATIVE ART EXPERI-ENCE, University of Wisconsin Press, Madison, Wisconsin, 1962. Although generally directed toward other facets of dance, this book should be read by every teacher and serious student of popular dancing. The theories and philosophies expressed by Miss H'Doubler should bring into better focus the frequently unused creative potential that it is possible to achieve through popular dancing.

Lisa Lekis, DANCING GODS, Scarecrow Press, New York, New York, 1960. One of the most comprehensive writings in English on the backgrounds of the dances of the Caribbean islands. Includes an extensive bibliography of additional articles and published material on that area.

BALLROOM DANCE MAGAZINE, 268 West 47th Street, New York City. Published monthly, this magazine devotes itself to all aspects of popular dancing from teen-age fad dances to the favorite and standard old timers. Informative articles by dance authorities, reviews of current record releases, and news of dance events and schools are included in each issue. A *must* for everyone interested in popular dancing.

INDEX

PB-001051.2
SIC-17

PB-0010542
510-17

30469

L. M. HODGES LIBRARY
WHARTON COUNTY JUNIOR COLLEGE
WHARTON, TEXAS